ADVANCE PRAISE

T0307445

"Jim was extremely helpful in guiding me to a position that was a perfect match for both employee and employer. Jim really made me think of different strategies heading into interviews, which paid dividends long after the interview was over. Jim was a great asset throughout this process."
Ken Seubert, Market President First National Bank Chippewa Falls

"Jim excellently presents the art of the interview in this book! Prepare and use these strategies, not only for your career development, but for every give-and-take conversation in your social network as well. This could change your life!"
Judith Weaver, Former R.N. and Social Worker

"This is what you need to know to close the deal."
Jim Brickner, CEO, Brickner's Park City

"This book will change your perspective on interviewing for the rest of your life."
Jeff Bean, President CEO, Beaver Chips Architectural Design Antigo

"*Interview Strategy* isn't just a handbook on interview preparation; it's a manual for your career."
Guy Allen Smith, Truck Driver

"In my 22 years of interviewing in the medical device field, I have never seen a book this thorough in preparing the candidate for a verbal exam, which is the interview."
Mike Sodini, CEO, Verify MD

"This book focused my attention on what was important to me, and helped me keep it in the front of my job search."
Dan Hinterlightner, Teacher, Merrill School District

"This is the most comprehensive book in interviewing I have ever seen. There is nothing to fear in an interview after you read this."
Dooner Hoffman, Owner, Hoffman Construction

"It's clear Jim's been through a lot in life. He has forged a mastery of communication and shares it with us so we don't have to crawl over the glass that he has."
Jim Slewitzke, Press Operator, Linetec

"This book is incredible. Two thumbs up. Way up."
Chelsea Trinker, Medical Librarian, Wausau Hospital

"I have no hesitation in affirming this book would be the difference in someone being hired for employment. Few self-help books I have read ever tap into such detail about human interaction. I found myself nodding my head in agreement repeatedly because I had experienced precisely what Jim describes in his book. Easy to read and inspiring. Jim's passion for interview preparation jumps off the pages. The secrets revealed in this book will do more than help someone achieve their dream job, it will help them achieve their dreams."
MGySgt John J Purcell, (Retired),
Career Recruiter, USMC

"Successful interviewing appears to be a dying art. As a high school principal I have sat in on a thousand interviews – some were inspiring, more were concerning and, unfortunately, most have been unmemorable. Jim Finucan successfully brings together a strong theoretical foundation, years of professional experience and valuable street smarts into one, easy-to-read and important resource. *Interview Strategy*, with its pages of sage wisdom, engaging stories and practical tips, is a must read for those looking to separate themselves from the pack through the interview process."
Shannon Murry, High School Principal,
Merrill High School

"There is no better book on interviewing. It's helped me conduct interviews as well as interview."
Rachel Hahn, Manager, Ballyhoos restaurant

"This is book is a guide for employment conversation, a roadmap for a career destination."
Ike Mattson, General Manager, Victory Lane

"As an attorney with 25 years of experience I find the methodology of questioning in this book to be helpful in my day-to-day work."
John Schellpfeffer, Schellpfeffer Law office

"*Interview Strategy – The next move is yours* is a must read for anyone that wants to further understand how important it is to manage one's own career. The book is a fast and easy read that takes the reader on a journey to better understand all the emotions, ups and downs of that roller coaster we call our career. Jim Finucan masterfully illustrates how our career choices and aligning a job function with our strengths and personality type is essential to our life and career happiness. More importantly, the book helps empower the career-minded reader to take action and educates regarding the complex process of interviewing, negotiating, resigning and starting the next level of your career!"
Jeremy Sisemore, CEO and Chief Marketing Officer, ASAP Talent Services

"This book makes me excited about grabbing the gold ring on this merry go round of careers and life. With the average person changing jobs/careers seven times in their lifetime, everyone should read this. Jim lives a passionate life. He lives what he preaches. This book is a treasure trove of inspiration and practical tips to help you have confidence in taking the next step."
Deirdre Worrell, Owner, Audiologist,
North Ridge Hearing Company

"I've never read a book that gave instructions on how to recognize and create opportunity until I read *Interview Strategy*."
Jay Schlueter, CEO, SGS Environmental Contracting

"Interviewing is a lost art; this book will steer you in the right direction."
Stan Janowiak, CEO, The Sawmill Brewing Company

"There are things we touch in life that have the power to change the direction of our lives. This book is one of those."
Dieter Bartz, Registered Nurse,
Lincoln Hills School for boys

"This book is a must read for anyone involved in a job search or wanting to advance in their career. Jim Finucan provides insight into the job search process that only someone with his extensive recruiting experience would know. It's great that someone who actually finds people jobs is willing to share his expertise. *Interview Strategy* is filled with stories, examples and specific ideas that will provide great results. I would highly recommend this book!"
Barbara J. Bruno, Sales & Recruiting Expert, Trainer, Speaker, Good as Gold Training, Inc.

"Jim has taken his years' worth of experience in recruiting top executives to help you bring your career aspirations to the next level. His use of humor and real-life examples shows how you can excel in any type of interview."
Nicole Johnson, VP Marketing & Innovation, PCCU

INTERVIEW STRATEGY

THE NEXT MOVE IS YOURS

JIM FINUCAN

Published by
LID Publishing Inc.
31 West 34th Street, 8th Floor, Suite 8004,
New York, NY 10001, US

The Record Hall, Studio 204,
16-16a Baldwins Gardens,
London EC1N 7RJ, United Kingdom

info@lidpublishing.com
www.lidpublishing.com

A member of:

Business Publishers Roundtable

www.businesspublishersroundtable.com

Printed in the United States
ISBN: 978-0-9987278-0-6

Cover and page design: Caroline Li

INTERVIEW STRATEGY

THE NEXT MOVE IS YOURS

JIM FINUCAN

LONDON   NEW YORK   SHANGHAI
MADRID   BARCELONA   BOGOTA
MEXICO CITY   MONTERREY   BUENOS AIRES

For Brandon, Connor, Leah and Kyle
God made you so that the world
is at your command.
Now go get it.

"In preparing for battle I have always found that plans are useless, but planning is indispensable."

– Dwight D. Eisenhower

CONTENTS

INTRODUCTION

Exposure decides your life. This principle is a fulcrum for the ideas and philosophy behind this book, which will help you to look for a career that fits your goals.

I spent my career in high pressure environments and was the sole provider for my family, my wife and four children. I learned skills that would serve me well and competed with aggressive salespeople in 'do or die' situations. Like you, perhaps, I withstood intense pressure from all sides, beside many workers who operated like me, doing what they felt was the best they could under the circumstances.

Often, as I would reflect on my options, I knew that I wanted something more but I had no idea how to obtain it. I stumbled from job to job and learned how to outperform those around me and learned that this was my only guarantee of employment. Although I barely graduated from high school, I knew how to work hard and focus my attention on one thing for an extended period of time. In fact, I loved focusing and working hard, since this would provide me with an escape from the pressures of life.

What I didn't realize is that it was a waste of effort to appease abusive bosses and give my best to companies who only took it and demanded more. For too long I wasted years of my professional life because I believed I could stay still, and hide from disaster, rather than go out and earn more money.

I worried about getting fired rather than admitting to the fact that I really shouldn't be working there in the first place. On the one occasion that I was fired from a job, it actually turned out to be the best thing that could have happened to me. When I look back over my own career, I see the need for a wise recruiter, someone who could have lifted me out of that stale environment and introduced me to a fresh group of faces, who could have utilized my skills to a new level and helped me achieve more goals.

Later in life, when I became an executive recruiter, I was able to witness the result of changing people's lives. I lifted them out of a life of drudgery and hell into a sunny plateau of happiness, recognition and reward. When following up with these people years later, I could hear the joy in their voices – joy that came from having made a career change at a valuable time in their lives. I was grateful to be able to provide hours of consultation that helped a candidate feel they were ready for change and could achieve success if it was pursued.

Change is a word that we have grown fearful of, sometimes just at its mention. Through our own conditioning, we have cowered too much of our lives under a rug of mediocrity, yet we are saddened at the reservoir of untapped talent rotting in our own potential. This causes a haunting feeling within us that the years are ticking away and we seem to be standing still, staying safe perhaps.

Interview Strategy is a book that is designed to assist people in evaluating options and improve their situation in order to propel into environments that will promote growth and prosperity. The thrust of this project is to empower anyone who desires it, with the knowledge and information to handle any interview situation. An interview is like buying a lottery ticket. It gives you a seat at the table where you get dealt a hand of cards and anything can happen. Your life can change in a moment, provided that you are prepared to express yourself effectively and convey your ambition and skills. If you can make the hiring authority understand your competence and potential, you can have what you are looking for.

This book can help anyone to enrich their life by positioning them with people who can recognize their potential and can help them live a life of satisfaction, achievement and happiness. So, study this book and pursue your happiness, and explore your freedom to enjoy life's abundance as this is the reward for realizing your potential. By incorporating even a few of the strategies described in this book you can propel yourself higher up for consideration in any interview process.

My hope is that *Interview Strategy* will give confidence to the uncertain, an edge to the skilled and assurance to those who feel that their skills are underused.

If you feel a clamouring inside that needs to be heard, but you don't know what to do about it, this book will help you. If you don't know how to search your industry for viable options that can change your life, this book will help you. If you feel that you wouldn't recognize a great opportunity if it came your way, then this book is for you. If you feel stifled by the environment that you operate in, or that the manager you work for is someone you cannot respect, yet you stay because you are not certain about how to approach the future, this book will lead the way.

There is a cascade of potential inside all of us. It requires hard work to cultivate and an inner template for comparing goals to the structures around us. A good career move is achieved when it is in accordance with goals and principles.

Read this book and step into the promise of opportunity because nothing is holding you back but your own insecurities. You are creating your own future every time you consider a new career move, evaluate its potential and make a decision based on factors that do not include fear. Join me in the eradication of limitations. Make a commitment to share your space and time with people who bring out your best and foster your full potential.

CHAPTER 1

INTERVIEWING — WHAT IS IT?

Merriam-Webster defines an interview as:

1:    a formal consultation usually to evaluate qualifications (as of a prospective student or employee)

2a: a meeting at which information is obtained (as by a reporter, television commentator, or pollster) from a person

  b: a report or reproduction of information so obtained

Having spent a great deal of my time and career in one sales position after another, there's a statement about selling that I once heard. It rang true and I remember it often: "Every time somebody opens their mouth to say something, they are selling."

With this in mind, it may then be said that every time someone asks another person a question they are, in fact, interviewing that person. Asking each other questions is how we express interest in each other. Joan Didion wrote: "We tell ourselves stories in order to live." We ask questions to connect and live through each other. When you answer my question, you respect me at a basic level. You acknowledge my existence and right to question you.

When answering questions, and certainly in interviews, it is important to always express the truth. Most people have a natural lie detector built into their subconscious minds. Our answers need to be as true as we know them to be, and should reveal self-knowledge and understanding. An answer that may seem trivial, but delivered from the heart, impresses the intuition of the receiver.

The interview should feel welcoming to both parties. It is a celebratory meeting of minds to share an interest, build professional relationships and qualify perspective personnel. It's something to be excited about and prepared for so that skills can be related with eloquence of expression, with an underlying spirit of gratitude.

From the employer's perspective, an interview can change the course of a company from struggling under pressure to bringing on talent that can launch the organization into a top position.

The place to begin, when considering your career, life and change, is your current philosophy towards interviewing and change. Fear of change is learned; change is uncomfortable and it breaks our rhythm of comfort – it can make you feel uncertain of the future. Security in any job is a lie. There is no security in life as everything is changing around us at any time; the illusion of security or regularity is paper thin and dissolves in a moment for all of us, at some time.

There is always danger in any comfort zone. You may be languishing in the familiarity that gives you a feeling of pleasure, but your mind will be weakening from the conditioning of this environment. Because you are content, feeling happy with your surroundings, you are not preparing your mind for change. The things you learned to get you here will not be enough to leverage you forward. The longer you delay preparing for future change, the more difficult it will be to absorb the reality. And when change comes you will be unprepared for it.

You can develop a sense of security with the know-how you have – this is a skill that can be transferred from job to job. A dedication to excellence that will be recognized by any employer is the only armour you have to wear while you go through the steps of fostering your future. An ability to read and train for skills in your industry is the only way to insulate yourself from the threat of being obsolete on a daily basis.

Your ability to survive and thrive is directly tied to your ability to handle change. To be a candidate in today's job market you must be ready to define and articulate the skills that you have developed over the years. You must be prepared to step into stressful situations and prosper. You must be able to work with difficult people and exact a predetermined result without falling back on excuses for nonperformance. You must know exactly what you want in your career and be prepared to pay the price to get it and not wait for it to drop on you, because it won't.

Employers are looking for this type of person with desperation. When interviewing, your philosophy will be revealed. Your perspective and belief system is the scope that you look through to weigh options, make decisions and project your future.

SELF-REFLECTIONS

What is your philosophy towards job searching, interviewing and change? This is a question you should ask yourself on a weekly basis. It is something that requires forging, remanufacturing and constant evaluation.

Does your current philosophy serve you or your employer? Can it serve both of you? It is the foundation of your thinking so it deserves some attention.

—————————— ACTION STEP ——————————

Interview someone you know, discreetly – they don't have to know this is an assignment. Take a special interest in their past, examine their reasoning and achieve a level of understanding by asking calm, gentle, probing questions.

Have an assuring amount of eye contact with them and listen to everything they say intently. That person will feel loved at the conclusion of the conversation.

CHAPTER 2

WHY
SHOULD I BE
INTERVIEWING?

*"Discontent is the first step in the progress of
a man or a nation."*
— Oscar Wilde

Ask yourself: "How can I engineer my career moves to get me to where I want to go?" This might prompt the question, "What do I want to do?" This is an excellent question and once it is answered, a path can be cut through any jungle.

Project forward:

In six years from now I will be making _____.

- To make that happen, I can seek a career move that will teach me the following skills _____.

- I am prepared to pay the following price to achieve the knowledge that will teach me the skills I need by

  _____.

- I need to read the following books to help me acquire knowledge and get an idea of how to grow in the most vital area of my career _____.

This book will trigger you to think about your career. Answer the questions and fill out the blanks to take the actions necessary to seek out what you truly want. If anything, you will gain satisfaction knowing that you made the effort to understand yourself better and perhaps the purpose of your life's work.

Asking yourself questions is a great way to guide your thinking. Let's look at a few challenging questions some might have about interviewing and career changes.

Why would I look at other options when I am perfectly happy where I am now?

Is happiness the pursuit of an easy lifestyle? It might be that you get along with your boss right now and, although you have not had a raise or promotion in years, your employer is nice to you. But is that all you want out of life? Is this happiness?

If you are a happy person in general, you will find a way to be happy. Your career is really not about being happy, it is about being fulfilled.

"Happiness is the realization of a worthy ideal," Socrates wrote. Is staying in a job where you are unchallenged, or taking on tasks that are beneath you just to stay safe, a worthy ideal? If you answered yes, you are in danger of being fired soon because of complacency. You are not challenging yourself to learn new skills and develop abilities to keep up with the changes in your industry. Complacent people are the first to be fired off like a rocket when cutbacks strike a company, or a new manager comes on board and notices a great deal of fluff in his department budget. You may feel your services to the organization are vital and that you are doing a great job, but it only takes a new manager who feels differently to turn your world upside down.

You should look at other options continuously because it is the only way for you to know what opportunities are around you. There is no other way to position yourself for success without examining what other companies are doing and what they might have to offer. In doing so, you will increase your personal power and immediately see yourself as a free agent. And that is exactly what you are – a free agent.

The structure of your happiness should be examined. What makes you happy in your current position? Is this happiness from external factors or internally carried? And because you are happy at this moment, would you be willing to walk away from a potentially great opportunity that could advance your career and benefit you? If so, is this a wise philosophy?

Set your happiness aside and examine your potential. Ask yourself if your life could be better with advancement. Now consider your current situation and estimate the advancement potential with your current employer. Realistically, how long could it take for you to get a raise or a promotion? Are you fully recognized for your contribution? Is there really no discontent? Challenge yourself on this premise.

Discontent is the first step in development. Many of us never challenge ourselves until we have to. But by developing the habit of challenging yourself before you have to will enable you to be prepared for the unexpected. The question should not be, "Are you happy?" but about knowing what would make you feel successful.

By frequently doing the things that make you uncomfortable, you find the ability to operate out of your comfort zone. This is a necessary skill to execute your interview strategy. "Skill to do comes of doing," wrote Emerson. Therefore, you must interview frequently, two or three times a week or month. Here you will learn the mastery of being interviewed, so that no meeting is wasted.

This is the only way to unlock your future and reveal your true, full potential to yourself.

What if I begin looking at other options and my employer finds out I am looking? The best managers are the ones who would never hold you back. A good supervisor wants you to be satisfied in your position. You are free to come and go from any job as you choose. If you do not exercise your freedom, you do not have it. The question above is one rooted in fear. If you live your life with the forces of fear steering you, your careers will suffer. Your limitations will be the walls that surround you and it only takes a little bit of fear to steer the soul of your boat so that it never wants to leave the harbour.

While ships are safe in the harbour, they were not meant to stay in the harbour. When you begin to hedge your bets and play to your fears, it won't be long before you surrender your freedom, your possibilities and your future to the phantom of the opinion of your employer. The most effective way to head off later professional regret is to prepare for it now. It is your responsibility to do this and no one else can do it for you.

What your employer thinks of your career search is none of his business. You work for a company and on pay day you are even. This organization or this company does not possess you and they have no right to govern your future. Your future is your concern. The company's direction is in the hands of the owner of the company. You might be stunned to know that your immediate supervisor is also looking at other options and interviewing for positions. What makes you think that this isn't the case? Assume this and feel immediate liberation from this concern.

Conversations with your employer – and I hope you are having them – should be about your future with the organization.

It is wise for an employee to exact information on what their supervisor perceives the future will be like for them. Talk of promotion, advancement and training should be regularly discussed during scheduled performance reviews. If these conversations are not taking place, why should your employer assume that you are not looking out for your own best interests? Why should it be expected that you will not explore your future to its fullest potential?

An employer should know the dreams and desires of their employees. At the same time, the freedom to search for what is best for all parties should always be welcomed. It is not a question of loyalty. By looking at other options you are not harming the company that you work for. Moving freely about your industry and examining competitors and sister industries will empower your spirit and psyche. As you do so, you will feel less frightened about your job security and the prospect of being unemployed. You will feel more confident as you explore options because freedom is defined as the ability to act. So, act and be free.

The book, *Topgrading*, by Bradford D. Smart explores the philosophy of a corporation that continually interviewed people to explore what talents were available. They didn't necessarily have an open position but the human resource people were advised to keep the doors open and evaluate the talent in the industry.

One of the things that CEO Jack Welch advised was to release the bottom 20% of performers in a company and replace them with people who were better in production. This revolving door allowed the flow of poor talent out of the door while the top talent marched in to replace them. Imagine the team a company could build with this strategy.

If companies are doing this, then why should employees not do so too? Through continuous evaluation of companies with potential positions you expose yourself to untold worlds of benefit. Your philosophy needs to evolve to keep up with the changing world. Your belief system should serve you and your career. In a way this is 'minding your own business' and not sacrificing your life at the altar of guilt.

That being said, minding your own business can also mean that you need not air it out in front of everyone around you. Be discreet in your job search out of courtesy but leave the guilt bag at a dumpster and know that it is normal and natural for you to explore your world. You should be conscious that as you change your viewpoint on interviewing and refrain from sharing this information with people that you currently work with, you should not assume that your co-workers are your trusted friends. Co-workers are often friendly and likeable people that possess a great sense of humour, exciting stories in the break room and hilarious comedy relief during times of tension. So, learn to deflect their questions with non-answers, or don't answer them at all when they prod you on why you are heading off to a meeting rather than having drinks at Freddie's Pub with them. There is no need for guilt, only discretion. There is no need to lie, only privacy. There is no need to get defensive, only take care in your communications. If word gets out, the fact that you are looking to excel your career could be resented by senior management. The only time your current employer should know you are seeking other employment is when you have just given your resignation notice.

Interview strategy is a methodology that enables you to give a hundred percent to your current position but does not limit your future options. Accelerating your career requires you to manage information and your actions so that you move discreetly with your plans and intentions. However, you should also be aware that there is an element of danger in practising interview strategy. If your employer find out you're playing the field and evaluating options, it could cause some tension. Some employers are threatened by this type of perspective and it could get you in trouble and cost you your job.

In the event that you are confronted by a supervisor about exploring other options, here are some ideas on what you could respond with. Remember, discussing your interviews is something you don't want to do with your boss. He won't understand.

"Just a minute, Alan, I would like to talk to you. Close the door please. Sit down. I understand that you have been speaking to some other print shops in the Cleveland area. Is that true?"

- If I were, would that be a problem? Why?

- Well Mr. Thompson, let me answer that question with a question. Have you yourself ever looked at another opportunity? Ever been called by a recruiter? What did you say? Do you ever wonder what might be out there? What is the long-term plan for my career with the group?

- Where did you hear that? What would be that person's motivation for saying such a thing?

- Well Mr. Thompson, I'm not really sure that question has anything to do with the performance of my abilities. Am I right?

- Why, should I be? Do you know something I don't?

- I'm not sure how to answer that sir, is there something you would like to say to me?

- That sounds like a personal question. Do we know each other that well? (Smile big)

- Before I answer that, can you relate to me what the policy towards employees who might have friends at competitor companies is?

More:

- That question reminds me of a story a friend of mine told me about an occasion when he had gone to pick up his friend for lunch at a competitor company. His boss had seen him going into the competing business and he got a raise!

When you are questioned in this way you have to provide an answer but, remember, you are the CEO of your own company, and this is one of your clients. Just one of them – you have others. You give everything you have to a job when you are there and outperform everyone around you. This gives you tremendous power to operate and manoeuvre your career to your advantage.

Another point to bear in mind when interviewing is that although you are in the process of interviewing for other jobs you may not be ready to leave your current job just yet. This is a valid mindset to have since interviewing is a skill we develop alongside learning to assess our situation in relation to our goals. It would be unwise to consider leaving your job without first securing another one to step into. For some people, making a change in their career is difficult because they like the company they work for, are fond of their co-workers and feel emotionally attached to them. Yet they look down the road professionally and there is no chance for advancement. Will they sacrifice their career to enjoy the people around them? Sadly, some do and over time people around them come and go while they continue to stay because they are comfortable.

Other people may find themselves in the situation where the writing is clearly on the wall. They run from one dramatic scene to another, putting out fires, having meaningless conversations with the same people that achieve no forward movement or results and they consider leaving but are frightened of change. Remember this quote by Warren Buffet: "Should you find yourself in a chronically leaking boat, energy devoted to changing vessels is likely to be more productive than energy devoted to patching leaks."

It is easier to leave a position that does not have a quantum of solace and leaves you exhausted and empty at the end of the day. When I spoke with a candidate with a secured offer of a more senior position and everything he had requested, the candidate told me: "The devil you know is better than the devil you don't know." I enquired as to where he had heard this expression and he told me that his father had mentioned it when he had told him that he was interviewing while being employed. I asked a few questions about his father and learned that he was a man who had made very few career changes and, as a result, had not achieved much in the way of advancement, but was always just content to have a job. Sadly, he had passed his low expectations on to his son. Decisions made out of fear are frequently made erroneously.

Career development usually takes place on the job and the working environment is actually an educational facility. Employers will train you and give you the experience you need to leverage your career. When you work alongside experts in the industry, you open yourself up to a new level of development by learning skills from them. Therefore, it is important that you choose the environment you work in carefully and ensure the people working beside you are role models that you can aspire to. Think about how you can work in the environment you want and gain exposure to mentorship opportunities with legends in your industry.

You should endeavour to view work environments as educational arenas. A good company will have a tremendous foundation of career development to pass on to employees. This benefit can be better than compensatory items.

In order to utilize the principles of *Interview Strategy*, it's necessary for you to see yourself as a student in any work system. No matter what your status is or where you happen to be, develop a sense of curiosity; cultivate a constant propensity to improve yourself and your situation by making a commitment to excellence in everything that you do.

Your goal should always be to evaluate, select and enter into companies where you can transform yourself into a revered and productive employee. Additionally, you should strive to master and improve your skills as much as you can gain from your current working environment and make it a part of you. Then, when the time is right, you can move on and take it with you to benefit others that you encounter on your journey. And also, you'll want to leave behind a wake of positive impression and improvement in the company that you exit.

Your career can involve some of the most important decisions you will make in your life, so it's important that you take care in your career choices. Listening to and talking with people who are considering a career change on a daily basis has enabled me to create a framework that can be utilized to examine the potential of a career change.

"Nothing is more difficult and therefore precious, than to be able to decide." Napoleon Bonaparte, Maxims 1804

We will begin with this writing exercise.

Where is the pain?

1. Write a paragraph about what is not comfortable at your current job. If you are comfortable and are considering doing exploratory interviewing, and this is fine, write that down here as well.

2. Give your current working environment a score out of 10 on the pain scale. ([1] I am blissfully happy here, and [10] get me out of here because the place is on fire.)

3. Get comfortable examining your situation and write down what made you take this job in the first place.

4. Would you like to be working here, doing the same thing, five years from now?

5. If you could change anything about your work situation, what would it be?
   • Does it need to be made now?
   • If so, how long will you need to make this change and who will you need to consult with to do this?

6. Can I put together a think tank of friends or family members who will listen to my thinking and help me evaluate my decision-making mechanism?

7. Schedule a consultative meeting with these people weekly to review your notes.

Your process should include a scheduled amount of time set aside for the review of factual information. Put around two hours a week in your diary to research companies, review job leads and work connections in your industry and outside to gain positioning.

When considering and making a job change, think about what is vital to your mental frame and your situation. If it is spending more time with your family, then you will need to make career decisions that favour positions which will keep you at home as opposed to being out on the road. So, your mental framework for this decision must keep what you hold dear first and foremost.

Next, look at where you are now. Ask yourself why you decided to work where you do now and examine your own decision making mechanism to date. Compare your decision to someone you know who made a different decision and is in a different spot.

Look over your statements written earlier with your BS meter on high. Do all facts and feelings still hold true? Are your concerns a passing emotional discomfort that seeks only an outlet for other dissatisfaction that is not career related?

Ask yourself questions about your skill level and job performance. Challenge your own potential with a reflection on the amount of training you've had and the results you've exacted. Look hard at your own track record of success. Where have you done well? Where have you failed? Examine yourself now because as we begin to place you in front of hiring authorities, they will be looking at you and will know who you are. "To thine own self be true," wrote Shakespeare – take his advice in interview preparation.

Purchase a notebook and take a piece of masking tape. Make a label for the front of the notebook and write INTERVIEW STRATEGY on it in big block letters and stick it across the front of the notebook cover, dead centre. Then write the date on it.

This notebook is for storing thoughts to be reviewed later. After each interview, there are several questions that you will answer while the meeting is fresh in your mind. Logging these thoughts will assist to critique the interview now and later. These thoughts will provide valuable feedback as you look for ways to improve your strategy, thoughts and direction.

These questions are:

1. Name of the company _____ date _____
    location _____.

2. What I know about the company?
    _____

3. What attracted me to interview with them?
    _____

4. Who I met with _____ title _____
    length of the meeting _____.

5. How was the chemistry?
    _____

6. Tough questions I was asked?
    _____

7. What I thought went well?
    _____

8. What could have gone better?
    _____

9. Do I want the job? _____
    Why? _____

10. Is this a move forward in my career?
    _____

11. If I want the job, what offer am I hoping for?
    _____

12.   What is my walk away number?
      _____

13.   These are my concerns _____.

14.   This is how long it will take to commute to the job
      _____ which means a total number of hours of
      road time in a week going to and from work _____.

15.   Feedback from Hiring Managers: Follow up results:
      _____

——————— ACTION STEP ———————

Take a ten-minute nap. Find a place where you can lie down in a dark and quiet place and set your alarm to go off in ten minutes. Use the first two minutes of the nap to bring your heart rate down and focus on relaxing the base of your neck. When the ten-minute alarm goes off, get up and face the rest of the day.

Practice this daily until you achieve expert level status. As we look at increasing pressure on ourselves for performance, it is important to be able to bring down the heart rate and get rest to power through a busy day. The nap is your answer to dumping stress, ditching fatigue and furthering your day.

You will feel sluggish at first when you achieve sleep, but half an hour later, you won't believe how good you feel.

CHAPTER 3

YOU ARE SELF EMPLOYED

You are the president of your own personal financial services corporation. Currently you may be leasing your time out to your employer (or client) but they certainly do not owe you a job. Not any more than you owe them your future. This contract can be broken by either one of you, at any time and for some of you reading this, it should have been broken a long time ago. If that last sentence hit you hard, think about how you could have lived a better life had you made such a change a few years ago.

What would you be doing if you could do anything you could dream of? You have decided to work where you are and that is good, but your future is your own and it is your own responsibility. What are you going to do about it?

Have you sold yourself short because you have been worried about not finding another job? Taste the bitter bread of regret if you must and let it stir a desire in you for change.

Change is good. What if your employers should find out that you are interviewing? If they are wise and you are productive, rather than fire you, they should exercise the strategy of employee retention and invite you to sit down to discuss your raise.

As the CEO of your own personal services corporation, are you really leasing your time out to the best contract or do you need to speak to some other companies? As a recruiter, I would call people and present options from their industry to them. I was always amazed when educated people would cut me off and tell me they were happy where they were without knowing what ideas I was about to pitch to them.

That being said, as a small business owner you have some responsibilities. Just as many small business owners do, you must train yourself continuously. Many corporations have budgets to train their employees and you must do this as well. It is not your client's or employer's responsibility to do so. Training yourself well will prepare you for an interview question like, "Did you spend any of your own money to train yourself on any industry knowledge in the last year?" Of course you did. This is a responsibility you would not leave to anyone, and because no one owes you anything, you took charge of your own education. This will help you to be considered as a top candidate in the process. You have initiative.

Your performance review is very important. It shows that your current client regards you highly and is satisfied with your performance and potential. The review may mean that training or development is required in certain areas of your profession. If we take the view that we are self-employed, we need to see how important it is to have a plan with goals for the next quarter, the next year, and the next five years. These plans are written and may or may not lead to an immediate career or job change, but frequently reviewing this plan will help you to stay ahead of the curve that way. It will help you to spend more of your time thinking about the future and what you want from it.

This perspective will serve you well as you interview with other companies. It will show that you are someone responsible for your own future and confident in your past, with no need to be apologetic. Believing strongly in your own independence will give you a sense of self command and you will radiate with confidence. And this confidence will be real because it was forged the only way it can be, through preparation.

But I worked so hard to find this job, and it was difficult. Why should I go through the struggle of interviewing

and stressing over a potential position that I don't even know I want?

Your reaction to the interview process needs to be controlled. We control our feelings by controlling our thoughts. When you found this job, perhaps you hadn't considered the fact that you are a CEO, you considered yourself as someone who was seeking employment, that is to say, you wanted to be taken in, cared for, supported, directed and harboured. In return you were willing to trade hard work, subservience and hope to get a raise so that you could, in essence, survive.

The fact that you are employed currently will assist you in being able to evaluate options without the spectre of desperation on your shoulder. When in desperate circumstances, it is easy to make bad decisions, overlook warning signs and be distracted by your situation and not ask the right questions. Equally, it is vital that while you feel comfortable in your situation, your antenna is up, and you are exposing yourself to possibilities.

Also, you will need to change your philosophy towards interviewing significantly. You will need to welcome the pre-tension of the interview until you grow accustomed to it. Do the thing you fear and the death of fear will be the result. Smile at your fidgeting fingers as you wait in the reception room. Feel the dump of adrenalin and relish it. Let your senses get heightened and turn the jitters into a type of excitement that will mutate the nervous energy into enthusiasm for the future and unharness the potential within you.

The samurai had a saying: "Welcome your enemy and send him on his way." This expression, to me, means that you accept the terms of the contest and are a willing player of the game. And it is all a game. Then the only question is, are you winning or losing? Only you can determine the answer to that. And don't be too hard on yourself on the decisions you have made in the past. It doesn't matter where you have been; it only matters where you are going.

It may require lots of interviews so steel yourself against your own nerves, complacency or lack of ambition and get ready to schedule some interviews, at least two a week, at first, whether you feel like it or not. The best way to predict your future is to create it, so don't short change yourself on one of the most important activities that will determine your future. And you can only create it by exposing yourself to options. Give yourself permission to do this and then, because it is so vitally important, do it and do it well.

In developing your interview strategy, think about what you would like to achieve in your career search. What would you like to gain from working all day? When you make a change, would you like advancement? If you like managing people, and see yourself as a leader because you give direction well and are charismatic, this could be a goal.

Perhaps in your next move you would like training and education; a degree from a university. Some positions offer developmental training and pay great expense for their employees to attend seminars and learn new skills in order to bring that value full circle for the company and their fellow employees.

Perhaps a career change for you is to enjoy life more with flexible free time. Some sales positions give free rein of scheduling work hours and time for their employees, allowing you to set your own hours to achieve goals outside of work.

Moving forward to you might mean more money – sure everyone wants that, but be prepared to answer the question: "What makes you worth more money?"

Consider this quote from José Ortega y Gasset:

"We distinguish the excellent man from the common man by saying that the former is the one who makes great demands on himself, and the latter who makes no demands on himself."

So, what demands have you placed upon yourself to prove that you have the excellence required to demand a higher salary? Are you ready to be examined on this point?

As a recruiter, when I reach out to a perspective candidate and talk to them about their career goals, they often say, "I'm comfortable here." It is human nature to be at ease but this may cause great pain later.

I know of a bank vice president who waited ten years to be promoted. He believed that he was going to be made president and waited patiently. But when the position become available, the bank hired someone from the outside, believing that the vice president did not have the ambition necessary to run the bank. The vice president was mortified, felt deceived and tricked into wasting ten years of his life. But he was wrong – no one owes anybody anything and his career was always in his own hands. In reality he had sold ten years of his life in exchange for comfort and his self-deception had prevented him from considering other options, making him believe that he was in the right spot. I know because I tried to recruit him for a president position in a competing company, and he wouldn't listen. In the end, he felt that his employer had lied to him; in reality, it was all his own doing, as our careers always are.

Comfort is a lie. It is the enemy of accomplishment. Comfort wants you to stay in this place where your friends work and tell jokes and laugh in the break room at lunch. Comfort will cause you to sacrifice your ambition of management, leadership and financial security and trade it for a mere pay cheque.

By following short-term comfort desires, you will put aside your long-term career direction. By standing still you will do more damage to your career than you would do if you took a chance to move forward. What looks worse, someone who moves around a bit or someone who stands still and is doing the same job for fifteen years, with no career advancement? Which one would you hire?

Your resume could use some moves. Gone are the days when someone gets a job, stays there for a lifetime and gets a gold watch. Companies are purchased, consolidated and restructured these days on a daily basis. If direct steps are not taken, you will end up standing in the past, 20 years will rush by, and then a realization will strike you that life passed you by while you hid from it. Your profession will discard you because you haven't kept up your skills or learned new ways to develop – you'll end up obsolete and bitter, blaming others for your decisions.

Following the advice presented and preparing well will help you to lead to your desired career. You can begin by preparing for an interview.

INTERVIEW PREPARATION

How well do I listen? This is an important self-evaluation that all of us should do on a weekly basis. Very few people listen well. It takes focus and concentration. It requires you to care about what someone else has to say. We have to forget our own interests, cares, worries and dodge our interior monologue to give attention to someone else. Listening is a basic expression of love. When you listen to someone, you give them validation and help improve their self-esteem.

Listening is an important skill that allows you to show kindness and love to your children, parents, spouse and every person you meet. It is a way to build a bridge to a stranger and make them a friend. It is a way to diffuse the rage of an enemy or the beginning of convincing someone to change their ways or agree with you on an important issue. It is the first step in mastering the interview. Your ability to walk into a room, perhaps face a panel of hiring authorities and decipher what they are saying, and respond to the crux of the questioning.

An expert response to a question always starts with a strong understanding of what the question is and, if it is not clear, requests for the question to be rephrased or for more information to be requested. It is important to comprehend what the interviewer is probing for before a response is given. In the case that you do not, the only response to give is: "I'm sorry I don't understand the question." And there is never any shame in giving this response at all.

The basis of the interview is a comprehension of shared ideas. To prepare for the interview is to quiet the nervous tension within you and enter with a silent mind that can flow and respond to the energy in the room. When listening during the course of the conversation, it's important that you don't let your mind wander and always wait for the person to be done speaking so that you can respond.

Responding to questions truthfully results from listening well. Once spoken, the truth has a ring to it that pleases the ear of the listener and makes them trust you. There is no right or wrong answer because the interview is a discovery and an exchange of ideas that seeks to find a match. Speaking the truth is your most powerful tool in any interview, and your ability to use it stems from the ability to listen attentively, without interrupting people. Practise the art of listening whenever engaging in conversation because it will truly set you free.

———————— ACTION STEP ————————

Listen to a story from someone and keep a mental outline of the topic. Respond to the story with three questions that relate to each topic you mentally bracketed to convey understanding and interest.

CHAPTER 4

RULES OF THE KNIFE FIGHT

"It's not wise to violate the rules until you know how to observe them."
– T.S. Eliot

Let's first think about physical appearance in an interview. This is not the time to reject the social norms of society, throw off the shallow perceptions of the world and revolt against those who judge others based upon their appearance by shocking them with your dress down demonstration. This is the time to dress well so that you stand out in the process for the right reasons and your dress style actually blends. You want to be remembered in the interview for your abilities, not your outrageous clothing choice.

Men should wear a dark suit, white shirt, classic red tie and shined black shoes with black socks. Every time, always, with no exceptions. Men, you have one uniform, wear it on every interview, a suit. If requested to show up in business casual, leave the blazer in the car and walk in wearing a shirt and tie with black trousers, black shoes and black socks. That is as far as you dress down. And women should dress professionally – a dress, a skirt or a pants suit, something sensible.

Your conservative dress style shows that you understand conformity, can fit in and are not trying to make a personal statement with your clothing, as this is not high school. Your clothes don't have to be expensive; they just need to give a professional appearance.

Equally important is your posture. With a straight spine and shoulders back, you project confidence and discipline. Hanging our meat on our bones takes constant practice and, when done right, delivers the message that you are a person of self-mastery and discipline. Keeping physically fit and mentally sharp for the meeting will do as much for you as being prepared for tough questions.

As what we are speaks more loudly than anything we can say, with a little practice you can enter the room and command respect and make everyone feel at ease with your manners and class. Your personal presentation – the way you dress and the way you carry yourself will not get you the job, but it will allow you to interview with your skills and not be eliminated for the wrong reason.

Next, take a fresh look at your résumé, print it off and take a pen to it. The résumé gets you the interview. It is used as a tool during the interview as well. It identifies your education level, experience and personal interests. It provides the outline used by the hiring authority for the direction of enquiries. The document deserves much attention and to neglect it is a mistake.

Grab a hold of your résumé and cut out the fluff, the bullet points and the extraneous words. Focus on your successes and the training you have received. Mention nothing that is not specific to an accomplishment. Under your name, address, email address and phone number, jump right into your work experience – starting with the most recent first and working back. For each position you have held, be sure to make it clear where you worked and what your title was there, the dates you started and if you are presently there. Beneath that, list your duties, responsibilities and achievements. This is where you brag.

Towards the bottom, list your education, extra training and online courses you are taking. With regards to education, your résumé should show that you are truly a self-starter; you take responsibility for this and actively participate in it.

Updating your résumé is something you should do every few months. It's a living document that is constantly changing and improving. The very act of doing this is something very cathartic. It makes you evaluate your past and gets you thinking about your future. It leads you to assess your strengths and will help you to prepare for change.

When a potential recruiter looks at the document they can learn many things about you: whether you are self-made or not, or whether you succeed in your accomplishments or move on to other things before seeing them through. A study of your résumé will reveal your values, upbringing and work ethic, but most of all it will reveal your habits. People who are successful have habits that make them that way. No one gets lucky; no one gets anywhere they are by chance of a roll of the dice. We live in a meritocracy; all things are earned and paid for in one way or another. It cannot be any other way.

So, if someone is looking at your résumé and understands you have a college degree from Louisiana State University, they may ask you how you paid for this school. The answer to that question can be very impressive or it may not, but give thought to how you would show your habits and background in the response.

According to the *Dubai Chronicle*, men speak about 7,000 words a day and women speak about 20,000. We are raised asking and answering questions on a daily basis, but does this mean we prepare and think about how we answer questions?

Sometimes people answer a question that they think they heard, rather than the question that was actually asked. Remember, if a question comes to you that you do not understand, state that you do not understand the question. Ask for clarification and in your *Interview Strategy* notebook make sure to capture the question that confounded you and everything you can remember about the experience. It may seem horrible now but when you review it in a few weeks you will find it very useful.

When a question is asked, listen carefully to the words and aim to understand the crux of the question. "Tell me the sales figures from 2013," you may be asked. To fly off on a tangent about the challenges you had, and dragging out an unsolicited story, is not recommended. A straightforward question warrants a straightforward answer.

"I achieved 80% of my goal by June and the rest by November. I added three new clients and worked through an IT conversion at the same time. I had a good year." When answering the question directly, don't miss the opportunity to inform the interviewer about your strengths and achievements, just in case he or she is not a skilled interviewer and does not know how to draw that out of you.

While it is true that compound questions are used in courtrooms to confuse witnesses, they are also frequently used in interviews, sometimes inadvertently, or sometimes deliberately. Compound questions are used for a number of reasons:

1. The hiring manager wants to know if the candidate can listen to abstract communication. If the candidate answers the first question but forgets to address the

second part, or the third, it may indicate a low level of perceptibility.

2.   The question touches on two opposing ideas and observing which one the candidate focuses on may reveal his or her passion.

To be safe, address each point to the question with a systematic response. This gives you a chance to highlight your skills and leave the small chat for later over coffee. We've got work to do here!

For example, you could be asked something like: "How do you manage your week, plan your days and find time to be the President of the Rotary Club?" When you hear this question, you may initially wonder if it is about planning your week, your days or would he like you to discuss Rotary? Does he want you to talk about how busy you are and where you find time to volunteer? Does he want to hear about your planning skills?

Your answer should be something like: "Planning my week is all based on the goal I have set, prioritizing my tasks and working all my critical activities into my timed schedule. I check what I am doing with a Wednesday accountability session. My daily plan is usually structured to time my day to the quarter of an hour with first, high level activity. nd I especially enjoy being the Sergent at arms of the Rotary Club on Tuesdays."

To answer compound questions, sometimes you may find it is necessary to set up your response. If your answer allows you to hit on a strength of yours, thank the hiring manager for asking the question. You can use an approach like: "To answer that question, I will need to let you know about my background training in analytics and my skill in attention to detail ...”

Because compound questions require a lengthier response, give yourself permission to extend your answer so that you nail all parts of it and return to the premise. If the answer was longer than you expected, don’t be ashamed to ask: “Did I answer your question?” It is better to be clearly understood in this instance than to leave it unanswered.

If the interviewer asks: “Take me through your daily routine,” what he or she is looking for is not a rundown of your duties and responsibilities and how you handle certain details, but an idea of your habits. Be prepared for this by stating what time you get up in the morning, what projects you undertake at home before leaving for work, your daily exercise routine, etc. Then go through your workday and list out all of the responsibilities and challenges, and touch on the skills that make you good at what you do. In this rundown of your day, also mention the victories you have obtained, the changes you have implemented and how they affected the daily operations of your schedule.

Wrap up your day with a description of how you assess your own level of achievement on a daily and weekly level, where you store it and how often you review it. Then move right into the end of the day. People who accomplish goals routinely do not spend lots of time watching television at night and couldn’t tell you what happened on *American Idol*. Do you play trumpet for the city band and practise in the evening? Do you read non-fiction books for an hour before you go to bed at night? Do you play racket ball at the local health club and gain a great deal of community connection from that? This should all be included in your answer to that question. As it is general, make your answer specific and use it as a platform to convey your developed sense of focus and reveal your vision. Try to keep it short and note that by using a good selection of words and tonality you can deliver a compelling response that will effectively reveal your mind set and clarity of focus. This can't be done while running off at the mouth about nothing.

When the interviewer asks a vague question, it is a test to see where you take the question. You can take the bait, if it leads you to your passions and strength, or ask for more information.

"So, tell me about yourself."

"What area of my background would you like me to go into first?" This response is better than stumbling around in the dark trying to guess what the interviewer would like to hear. But don't be coy when you answer this way. In general, people do not like the answer to their question to be a question so be tactful.

"Tell me a story."

"I have a million of them, what kind of story would you like to hear?"

Now if you can take this question into a good dissertation of a certain set of skills that you want the hiring manager to know, then launch into it. And remember to always smile and genuinely enjoy yourself.

The general question can be your friend and a chance to lead into what you want to tell the hiring manager, or it can be a trap that has you blurting out strange things from your past as you wonder what the hell you are saying. It's all about preparation. But be careful, the interview is not a time where you should talk about your past dark secrets. Remember that some of the best teachers in life are our past experiences, especially the mistakes we have made. Set aside your emotions for a moment and embrace the experience for the sake of learning.

ACTION STEP

Call your last two past employers and ask them if they would write you a letter of recommendation. Do this and listen to everything they have to say without interrupting them. Then, regardless of what happens, thank them emphatically and mean it.

CHAPTER 5

SELF-EXAM IN PREPARATION FOR THE INTERVIEW

"It is better to fail at your own life than
succeed in someone else's."
– André Gide

Interview Strategy is designed to develop you with a high level of self-knowledge and awareness through enquiry. Look hard at your résumé for faults. Not just typing errors or technical issues, but look at the moves. Are you proud of all of them? Did you succeed in your own goals at each place you worked? What were your goals? Is the company glad you worked there? Would they hire you back?

Look at the wake you left behind. Was it joyous? Are the people you encountered, from your co-workers and supervisor to the owner of the company, glad for the experience? Or did you leave behind you a blood trail?

I accept responsibility for all of my actions and offer no excuse or hide from anything. Let's set that deep in your mind and discuss it when probed on your principles. Principles will come through in an interview. In fact, you can't hide them when people check a reference or examine your work history.

But as you examine what you have left behind, you may find that in your past, you didn't achieve what was set forth. If this is the case, explain to yourself how you let this happen, with no excuses. Take responsibility for your part. You don't need to beat yourself up but it needs to be examined if it is never to happen again.

It doesn't matter where you came from. What does matter is where you are going. By charging forward with your foundation improved, you need not hang your head and project guilt at your past in an interview. Instead, you can explain how you have changed this thinking that caused the situation and own it.

Have you ever known a special sort of individual who was so kind and gentle that they never spoke an ill word about anyone? I have had the pleasure of knowing such people. And in the interview strategy method, you must become one of those people.

For you and me to become one of those people we must take a vow now that we will never speak negatively about anyone again. There are forces in this world that are like boomerangs – we send them out and they end up coming back home to us again. Negative energy and conversation works like that.

It is hard for you to look cool and composed as you whine about what happened at your last job and how everyone picked on you. Quickly, you can appear as someone who is undeveloped and doesn't take responsibility for his or her actions.

So, if you had a bad experience with a former boss, think of some positive things to say about that person and state that you had a difference of chemistry if you must – or state that you had difficulty working with that person, then say no more. The point will be taken. If the interview team presses, steer your comments to positive and honest statements that are innocuous and smile friendly. Here you demonstrate discretion and show that you can manage information and personal differences without airing them out all over town. This could show the interviewer that you are trustworthy and they respect you, knowing that if for some reason things don't work out well with you, you will at least have the decency to keep your mouth shut about it.

Any time any of us has a problem with someone, we should first ask ourselves: "What was it, within me, that caused this problem?" This is the first step in taking responsibility for whatever occurred. The company gave you a job and you took it – that makes for mutual liability in whatever transpires from there onwards.

How you feel about this situation will become prevalent to a skilled interviewer so it is critical that you feel at peace with your past.

Rather than try to figure out what is going on in the head of the interviewer, simply prepare to speak well of your past and the lessons learned. The interviewer can gain something valuable by studying how you make decisions. Avoid speaking of specific events but give words to underlying themes of difference in values, opinion or beliefs. Let's move on.

> *"Life is not a matter of holding good cards,*
> *but of playing a poor hand well."*
> – Robert Louis Stevenson

In order for you to make a favourable impression on a potential employer, and at the same time interview the company and employer as a perspective mentor, you must give some thought to your current situation.

What was it that drew you to the position that you are in now? There is a question of the chicken and the egg that is relevant for us all to understand. Did you choose this job or did the job choose you?

This question is more complex than we might think at first. Some readers might have targeted a certain profession, studied for it in a scholastic form and then plunged into it with bravado. Others might feel that they stumbled into their profession – are both of us wrong or both right?

A career choice will use your natural ability to communicate, ability to think in certain ways and ability to access the skills needed to perform required duties. What is important for you to understand, as you begin to be evaluated at new levels, is that you must know all of this about yourself. Then you must challenge them. All skills are learned and therefore learnable. So, what skills have you chosen to learn and what skills have you gravitated away from? Why? As president or CEO of your own company, ask yourself the questions that relate to your skill sets. In understanding what you are good at, and what comes naturally to you, you can determine if you have chosen a field that supports those interests? Should you target your weak areas with time devoted to development, or focus energy on accelerating the results of your strengths? Ride the horse the direction it is running. By exercising your interview skills, you will develop an ability to communicate your skills, talents and interest and you will find that you can knock on doors that might open an entirely new career path for you.

Be open to the possibility to not only change your job, but to also change your career. In developing your interview plan, be sure to include scheduling in interviews with people in totally different industries and professions. When you know what your skills are and can relate them to other industries, it may be possible to convince an employer that you are worth a chance and that they can train you in a new field. It will be up to you to prove that you are the type of individual who is worthy of such a shot. And then you must evaluate the offer to see if this is what you want.

To truly change your interview philosophy, it will be necessary to set goals as a daily ritual and this will require some time. For you to be able to answer the question: "Where do you want to be in five years?" you will have to think about that every day and practise articulating it to yourself. Writing down your one year, five year and ten year goals will drive them into your subconscious and allow them to flow out in an interview in a compelling and attractive manner.

A skilled interviewer will be analysing your vision, your ability to see yourself in the future achieving the dreams you set for yourself. This begs the question: "What is a vision?"

> *"A vision is a clearly articulated, results-oriented picture of a future you intend to create. It is a dream with a destination."*
> – Jesse Stoner Zemel

When someone is questioning your vision in an interview, they will be listening to how well you have prepared for the future. Be prepared to speak with a certain relish about where you are heading in your career, mention the steps you have taken to prepare, list all your jobs up to date and mention the things you have learned that are relevant to the overall picture.

The interviewer may ask: "Where do you see yourself ten years from now?" When he does, know that he is testing your vision.

"I will be the best SAP programmer in America one day. I will be in the top ten percent of earners in the information technology industry within the next eight years. I plan to outperform others around me while earning their trust and admiration. When the time is right and it suits my career I will move into a management role in the field and train and mentor others, as this is a strength of mine. One day I will own my own company."

The interviewer might follow up on this with: "How do we fit into that plan?"

"Your organization is known to be a top performer in the information technology industry and you are not afraid to train people and invest in their development. I know that from your website and talking to the people that I know who have worked here. I see it as a strong fit for both of us and I think once you see my potential, you will be glad you hired me. I can see a long-term fit here for me," you say and smile pleasantly.

Leaders have a vision of the future; it is one of the defining factors that must be present in any mentor, manager or CEO. People who can develop the ability to see into the future, imagine themselves being there, and look back from that future and make plans and implement strategies that will provide the framework for the necessary possibilities to achieve that success, are called visionaries. Develop your sense of vision by writing vision statements on your legal pad: "In five years from now I will achieve this level of career education ..."

The ability for you to discuss your potential is what this process is about. Prepare for it daily and it will manifest itself in real time before your eyes. By changing your philosophy about interviewing, your future and your potential, you begin to position yourself for advancement in such a way that there is no force on earth that can stop you from moving on and getting what you want.

For this philosophy to serve you, there are some basic practices that you must forge in your life, if you have not already done so. Because you are self-employed, you must strive to be a top performer in your industry. Working hard, offering no excuses for non-performance and exacting the results the job requires in any situation will need to be very important to you.

Anyone that is inherently lazy, disinterested or unable to work hard will not be able to enjoy the advantages and satisfaction career development can bring. So wherever you are, make that a priority now, make the current situation, even if you have decided to leave already, the best that it can be. Outperform everyone around you. If you have made up your mind you are leaving, leave well and give them something to miss.

A skilled interviewer will be looking into your background, your current situation and your mentality for achievements in your career. They will question you as to why you are thinking of leaving where you are because they will want to know if you are being driven out, or if you are driving yourself to excel in your field. They will come to know you by your work.

This does not mean that you have to have a perfect track record of never making a mistake, and it does not mean that you are flawless. But giving reason to communicate your desire for change will be vital, and it should not sound like sour grapes.

Conveying that you are looking for possibilities that utilize more of your potential will ring with truth. It should be clear to the interviewer what you are doing there and why.

So make sure that you prepare well for the question: "What are you looking for in your next move."

There is no book that you can read that will give you a verbatim response to that question. To spout someone else's candour will not serve you well. Prepare for this question by writing the answer several times as it comes to your mind. When you have completed five attempts, read them over then select one that sounds most like you. Then write it again. This action will clarify it in your mind and allow you to express it clearly and naturally in a manner that will not sound rehearsed. Speak it out loud and let your ears hear it. Does it feel true?

Conveying to a prospective employer why you are applying there must be clear to you, so that you can make it clear to him. Dropping the ball here could end the interview fast. If an interviewer cannot understand why you are looking for a change in employment, it will haunt him through the process.

—————————— ACTION STEP ——————————

Review the last four years of your career as though it were a movie rolling out before you on a screen. Let the interactions you had with co-workers unroll, examine your successes and think of the scenes where you learned a lesson. Remember the thrill of advancement and the congratulations of achievement and count those scenes. Did the movie thrill you? Did you cry? Did you laugh? (and that's worth a great deal). Were you angry and want your money back? Take responsibility for it all, because this show is yours.

CHAPTER 6

SPEAK TO YOUR STRENGTHS, JUST WHAT ARE YOUR WEAKNESSES?

*"What you do speaks so loudly that I cannot hear
what you say."*
– Ralph Waldo Emerson

"What's this 'we' business? Do you have a little rubber mouse
in your pocket?" This is a question that you can expect when
you answer questions with 'we' rather than 'I'.

No one cares what 'we' did; 'we' are not applying for the
position. 'We' are not in the interview, there is only you. It
is almost as though you are unwilling to take responsibility
alone for the things you have done, even the accomplishments. This could be because you have been told not to brag
or steal responsibility for work that a group did and it lays
latent in your mind, but it now springs out to sabotage your
chance of getting this job by undercutting your own accomplishments. The achievements that belong to the group will
be ascribed to the group, but you are not here to discuss the
group. You should discuss your own achievements.

Answering questions is something that you have been doing
all of your life, but that does not mean you are good at it.
Answering questions well is an art like anything you take
up and wish to do seriously. You should develop your own
technique of answering questions in formal settings.

Answering questions in a formal setting

A.   Paraphrase when necessary, but only when necessary:

1.   When addressing a compound question or a question with any rambling associated with it for a
length of time. Paraphrase subtly; grab the most

important point of the question and comment on it with one sentence before delving into the answer.

B.   Set it up if it requires it.

1.   "If I understand you correctly, you are enquiring as to my ability to produce results with my own accounting desk while I manage a team. I can relate my history at Anderson and Wesley where I maintained my position as a lead accountant while overseeing the work of four other staff members. In fact ...

2.   If you are going to answer with a story, "Let me answer that by relating an incident that happened with a customer of mine ..." Set it up by including the controversial points that make the situation tense, and the players that have something to lose. But keep it under two and a half minutes. Tops.

C.   Identify the heart of the question and speak directly to it.

1.   Try to limit your answer to four sentences. This will force you to be concise and stay on point.

2.   Give hard data, numbers and results and end it with mentioning any awards won, landmarks of achievement and things learned.

3.   Avoid saying 'we'; speak only of things that you were responsible and accountable for.

4.   Close it with an emotional connection if possible, touch of humour or enthusiasm.

Having a system of handling questions will assist in fielding, internalizing and responding in the interview, and give you an edge in dealing with nervous tension. Remember only you can convey the skills that you have mastered and it is imperative that you know how to do so.

In preparing to discuss your qualifications in an interview you need to be ready for this question: "What are your strengths?"

What a fantastic opportunity to express exactly what you have come here to talk about. This question is so basic in interviewing that if you are not asked it, it should be your desire to find a way to steer the conversation towards this topic and to stay on it as long as possible.

Perhaps you do not see yourself as a braggart, but this is the time to relate your abilities and articulate the very measure of what you have learned and accomplished. Be prepared to communicate how you have applied them to your career. To practise answering this question, take a note pad and write at the top 'My Strengths' and underline it twice.

List one that comes to mind, the first one, whatever it might be. For example, you may write something general like: "I communicate very well," then write down how you use that strength. "In my current position, I am the one who speaks up at meetings and identifies challenges that we face as a team and begins the process that moves us toward a solution."

On the next line down, write a sentence on how you believe you may have developed that strength: "I think, being the youngest of four children and growing up in a very verbal family, we frequently expressed what was on our minds and I learned early in life that ideas were valuable and by talking about solutions, life got better."

The next line down, write how you intend to develop that strength and continue to leverage it, as it applies to your career: "I have signed up for a class at the community college in public speaking and I have joined Toastmasters. I feel that if there is a chance in my career to sell a certain product or influence potential clients with a rousing tribute of a certain product, I hope to be the one to do it."

Now move down and write down strengths number 2, 3, 4 and 5. The more closely you can relate them to your industry or field, the better. Ask people who are close to you what they perceive your strengths to be, then write down their responses. The fact that you are writing down yours and other people's thoughts on your strengths will mean that they are more accessible to your mind in the interview, when you are slightly nervous.

Remember that you will be competing with all the others who are lined up in a waiting room interviewing for the same job. The difference between a candidate who can verbalize their strengths, confidence, self-knowledge and maturity well between one who cannot is dramatic.

The next question to follow, however, will be: "What are your weaknesses?" If there ever was a loaded question, this is it. This question is the proverbial rope to hang you with, and there is no good answer here. How can you sound confident and intelligent confessing your weakness to someone in a job interview where you could hope to be employed?

As a recruiter, I have heard at least 500 responses to this question. Candidates tell me they like to say, "I work too hard."

Or, "I don't know when to quit and sometimes an entire day slips away when I am on a project." Forget it. What you don't know is that the last candidate that didn't work out with the company felt that he worked too hard as well, only on the wrong project. Or you don't know that the last person they had to fire was also lost in the day, but the project he was so engrossed in was not one of great importance.

The best thing to do, when asked about your weakness, is let your mind go blank, look around the room stunned, and say: "I can't think of one right now." And hope the interview moves on or find a way to circle back to talking about your strengths.

"Come on, there must me something that you are not good at."

"I guess I am not very good at explaining my weaknesses in job interviews. You see, I am a very positive person and inherently I focus on outcomes that I wish to achieve so it goes against my nature to embellish on the negative. It tends to be a very dark slippery staircase for us all, wouldn't you agree?" Follow this comment with an awkward smile.

KNOW YOUR RÉSUMÉ

Yes, you wrote it but are you prepared to describe in detail any gaps in time, any short stays at companies, and are you ready to describe why you left each past employer? Spend some time knowing what your résumé is stating about you and what it isn't.

When a perspective employer begins to crawl through your past with the document you have provided, they are looking for inconsistencies in your responses, evasive answers or reasons for leaving past employment. A prospective employer is now moving into a different realm, not of qualification but of disqualification. Both are equally important to survive if you want to complete the interview process successfully. And a good interviewer will use both perspectives at some point in the conversation.

This could also mean that he or she has seen something they do not like and although they are smiling, a flag is up. Don't break stride in your answers or become fidgety or nervous but welcome the challenge. A potential employer who is asking you for the reasons you changed employment, is doing so for good reason. Hiring employees, spending time and money training them, only to later find out that they are not suitable for the role is a waste of money and time for any corporation and the interviewer will want to minimize such a risk. So, it is hard to say how many moves may be acceptable in a given time frame; an employer may have their own restriction on such behaviour. The important thing is not to get all shook up in the meeting when you are asked why you have moved three times in the last three years.

To prepare yourself ... start writing: "Why did I leave?" Answer the question for your previous three jobs and then examine your answers. And if you have had some moves, there is no need for apology. What is very important is answering questions about your past and why you made the decisions that you did. If you don't know the answers, then who does? Throw out worry about whether it sounds good or not. State the facts as beneficially as you can and let it lay where it may.

If you've improved yourself in those moves, mention it. If you've learned a new skill, developed in your profession in each of those moves, state that as well. Examine your thoughts about your reasons for change and rehearse them with a friend, until you can speak clearly and confidently about your own past.

"What specific traits do you possess that will allow you to take on these responsibilities extremely well?" The interviewer may ask you this question right out, or he or she may come at it from another angle. But they will be expecting you to answer this question in many forms. So, prepare for this question and the answer will feel natural. Pick four qualities that you have developed. Think about them, you have been developing since birth, but rarely think about articulating how you've progressed. Here are some examples:

1. On your notebook, write down the things you've finished. College, writing a book, an online language class, barber school, formal credit training or sales conferences are a few examples that may come to mind. Collect them on paper. Each time you write down what you have begun, struggled to get through and worked to completion; write down what you learned from it. And write down what was most challenging about it. Think of the obstacles that challenged you during that assignment.

2. Alexander Graham Bell wrote: "Concentrate all your thoughts upon the work at hand. The suns rays do not burn until they are focused."
   Think of times and accomplishments that have required a high level of focus, and write down how you were able to achieve this, how you developed that ability, what exercises did you use? What preparations did you take?

3. You will need to be able to explain your own source of motivation. Think of the ways you've outperformed your team mates, chosen challenging projects and were unintimidated by a looming deadline. Think of the selections you've made; the energy you've projected at goals and aspirations you have followed. Write them down on a sheet of paper going into detail about where this energy comes from by examining your motivations.

4. "Attention to detail is the religion of success." You too have lived your life with great attention to things that have made it possible for you to accomplish what you have thus far. Examine and write down three areas in your life that have required great attention to detail, how you learned them and how they've served you well.

Now, re-read the question stated earlier: "What specific traits do you possess that will allow you to take on the job?" and write down three answers for each of the four points above. Out of the three answers, which one is the best? Rewrite it until it is a fluid, well expressed statement and state it out loud to a friend or an empty spot on the wall. We will go into more detail on this technique later on.

——————— ACTION STEP ———————

Go for a run and spend the whole time visualizing your ideal future!

CHAPTER 7

MONEY SHOULD NOT BE A PROBLEM, UNLESS THERE IS NOT ENOUGH OF IT

"Money is only a tool.
It will take you where you want to go but
it will not replace you as the driver."

– Ayn Rand

Would earning more money from your current employer keep you in your position? If the answer is 'yes', then it is safe to say that your reason for leaving your current employer is fiscally related and this can be a very valid reason for leaving a company. But you may be susceptible to the counter offer when you try to resign. Sometimes employers make these offers to keep an employee with them. It is really the only thing they can do to try and keep you. This counter offer can be more money, it can be a new title, a supervising position, company stock, an administrative assistant, parking spot, you name it. It will be something that you have requested in the past but were denied, or something that they know you would have liked but they were not able to provide.

Your interview strategy will serve you well up until this point, but now your real motivations are tested. If there is any hesitancy, you will still be working there next month. This is the jumping point at the end of a diving board and now your resolve to take the plunge will be tested. In order to prepare to resign you must first prepare for the counter offer.

So, fast forward: you interview, meet a group of people with a great set up for your career, fall in love with the idea of this exciting change, receive an exciting offer, accept it, tell your friends and family about this bold exciting change in your life, then go in to resign. Rather than accepting the resignation, your current employer matches the offer and you end up staying. You realize two weeks later you made a mistake and you should have left the company.

The solution to this uncomfortable situation is to ask for a raise from your current employer as you begin examining your options with other organizations. If more money will keep you where you are at present, then you must ask for a raise in a professional manner. Only then will you be ready to handle the counter offer to stay for more money when you execute your resignation.

Asking for a raise is a business conversation. It must be done with the right person in the company. Here's a list of what not to do in the conversation when requesting a raise:

1. Don't use reasoning that is personal. The fact that your spouse is laid off, you need money to put your kid through college or your house needs a new roof is of no consequence to the company and quite frankly, none of their business and has no place in this important business meeting.

2. Don't whine or complain about working conditions, things you feel might be unfair in the company or bring up being slighted in anyway. Keep the platform of the conversation as positive as you can.

3. Don't bring up any co-workers who might have received a raise or are better paid than you for doing less work. Stay far away from any comparison unless you are simply using a national compensation range of pay, and even then have the documentation with you for reference and be prepared to leave a copy of it when you exit the meeting.

4. Don't nod your head habitually in agreement with the employer or say things that you don't mean. Every word should add to your position or don't speak it. Speak only when necessary to convey strength and confidence.

The reasons you give for this request should always be performance related and need to be focused that way. First, do your own performance review and be ready to show and explain how you have helped the company's bottom line through your efforts. Be prepared with figures and examples that show an increase in your performance since your last salary raise was issued. Show how your responsibilities have grown and accentuate your presentation with a graph or a chart of your performance level and how it has been profitable for the company. If you have helped mentor other employees or new arrivals in your group, bring that up now as well.

Make the point that your income has simply not kept up with your professional growth and cite any online classes you have taken at your own expense to improve your performance. Mention other certifications and seminars you have attended that have helped in your professional development.

The point that you need to make is that you are not really the same employee that you were when the salary you have now was issued to you. When you've completed your well-rehearsed presentation on why you would like a raise, and it included the exact amount of increase you are seeking, sit still and wait. This is not the time to be incessantly chatty; hold yourself erect and professional, even if you are quite friendly with your boss. Of course, the response you are looking for is, "Yes, here it is," and the raise issued. But if you receive a response that relates to your next scheduled review my advice is not to argue at this point. Make no counter point to this response, just listen attentively. Let the meeting conclude cordially and dismiss yourself professionally and return to your duties. But you have learned something very valuable by having this meeting. You have learned where you stand here, what your real value is to the company. You have been shown a glimpse of your future here and have explored all the opportunity there is to explore. And now you have seen the limitations and sometimes this truth can stare hard into your face for the rest of the afternoon.

When you have accepted the offer of a new position and walk back into that same office to hand in your resignation, the raise that you requested three months ago will suddenly be the presented as a retention package. But the time to buy you now, after you have found and accepted another opportunity is too late. Remember that once you resign you can never go back. That is a line you must never cross. Or you could end up meeting yourself coming back on the road in life.

Let's discuss how to bring up the issue of money in an interview. Only a few issues seem to cause more stress to an interviewee than the possibility of talking about compensation. I have met candidates who'd simply refuse to engage in the conversation about money because they felt that it was a private and personal matter. In one particular case, when I asked the candidate how he intended to get the salary he wanted if he didn't discuss it, he seemed stunned and replied: "Their job is to make me an offer."

Let's give some thought to the negotiation, as that is what an interview is. It is a business meeting to determine a possible fit of skill sets for a position and work out a financial arrangement and terms. Once the culture is a fit, and you are excited about getting the job for myriad reasons, the objective is to receive and accept an offer. So, if you are serious about making a career change, you must handle the money discussion with strategy. The question itself can come up at any time in the meeting. It can appear in the first interview, even if it is a phone screening, or at the final meeting between the candidate and the interview team. What is important is that you welcome the question at any time.

Compensation is not an emotional topic; it does not hold any judgment towards anyone nor does it classify you as a human in a caste system. It is a tax question that lines up people with organizations as a prominent and upfront qualifier.

You cannot expect to receive an offer of $130,000 with a job description that states the salary is up to $95,000 tops. This conversation is a way for both sides to qualify each other very quickly and it should come up early on to spare you from emotional investment into something that was not going to work out, but late enough for you to build good interview rapport. Sometimes, a company will stretch a compensation range if the candidate has exceptional qualifications, so it may be advisable to relate your skills sets before discussing the money question. The question of money could sound like this:

- What would it take to get you on board?

- What are your salary requirements?

- What range are you hoping for when we talk money?

- How much do you need to take on these responsibilities?

If the question feels unsettling, it is because it is unfair in its general premise. The interviewer is asking you to write your own offer and, as my candidate stated earlier, it is the company's job to write and extend the offer. The offer will reflect what you need to know about the company, a last chance for you to consider your gut feeling and to realize if this environment is the right match for you. The company will be watching you closely and weighing your decision-making skills once they present their offer to you. So you should avoid the pitfall of mentioning a number that is too high or too low for that matter; the answer is to simply state the number you are currently earning. This is a great time to reveal your entire package. It is information you want them to have, lest you run the risk of them embarrassing themselves by extending an offer so low as to not even match your current situation. The answers might sound like this:

"I'm currently earning $74,000 base and I earn a 10% bonus on base at the year end. For vacation I have 22 paid days off and have an ESOP plan that matches 4% of what I put in. That is pretty much the extent of my package, but this isn't all about money, I'm really looking for a great opportunity and I'm sure any offer you make will be fair."

This response is neutral and provides a reference point for the interviewer. They need to make a statement about how much they want you on board, how much your skills and abilities are worth and what the capacity of the organization is to recruit and obtain good talent. With their offer the employer shows its hand in its abilities, its selection process and the acumen for recognizing your skills and making a play to get you. It can be very flattering when done skilfully. All of this begins with you revealing correct and accurate information in the meeting.

The money question can sound like this: "What are your salary requirements?"

"Well, I currently earn $84,000 base and a 20% bonus annually. I am given 28 days of paid time off, and have three personal days I am assigned to use. The company puts a 6% contribution into my 401k plan and my insurance costs me $340 a month and has a $5,000 deductible." Speak these words slowly so you don't have to speak them again, as one of them should be writing this down. "But I'm sure any offer you make would be fair."

They wanted a reference point and you gave them one. Another option to end that statement could sound like this: "But it's not about the money, what I am really looking for is a strong opportunity." By telling them where you are at, they should know not to offer you less than what you are making. If they do, be ready to listen to the reasoning, looking for career advancement or education and training.

But the hiring manager may not be so ready to let you off the hook. Angry face plate might say:

"That's very coy; now tell us what you would like to see in an offer."

"If you are making an offer, I am open to hearing any offer you may have," you say and hold a pleasant, expectant expression on your face and have a feast of some eye contact with them all. A few things can happen here. They could make you an offer. In which case, you may feel compelled to give an answer because you just played a tough hand of poker, but you don't have to. It is generally accepted that once an offer is issued there is a time period of response that can be expected. In some cases, depending on the company, it could be as short as 24 hours or a week.

It is important that the company puts a deadline of acceptance as part of the extension of the offer. They have other candidates waiting in the wings who were ranking second to you.

Additionally, the interviewers may be put off by your refusal to confirm a pay package that you would accept. They may see this as you being flippant or evasive when it came to this vital subject. A way to prepare for this would be to explain why you are asking them to make this first and critical move.

The result could be that they will get back to you promptly with a dynamic offer that meets all the requirements of your career search. This happens when you sow the seeds of career orientation and goals into the interview.

If an offer is presented to you in the final interview or sent to your home or to you via email, you should schedule some quiet time and ask yourself some questions and perform these exercises. Ask yourself this:

- Money aside, do I want the job? Why?

- Is this a move forward in my career? In what way?

- Five years from now, will I be better off for taking this position? Why?

- What will my current employer do when I resign? (They will present a counter offer to stay, possibly match an offer from the competing company or exceed it.) If they should make me a counter offer to stay where I am, will I take it?

If you answer yes to the last question, you are not ready to leave your current situation and are only playing around here with this interview. And that is ok, as long as you know that this is what you are doing.

If, however, you answer that with money aside, you do want the job, and there is nothing that your current employer can do to keep you, you really are ready to leave and have found a position with a desirable company.

What will you accept and what will you turn down as an offer? This question should be lucid in your mind before you receive the offer, especially if it will be presented to you live at the conclusion of the meeting. It is critical to your negotiation to know what you want or what you certainly will not be able accept.

The average person moves for a 7-12% increase on their base salary. These are just, but what is vital is that you know what you will walk away from.

In general, if your demand for compensation is high, you are not that excited about the opportunity. In fact, you may even be hoping that it doesn't work out so that you can go back to the status quo and not have to bother with all this change stuff anyway.

On the other hand, if you are excited about working with dynamic brilliant people, and have found a position where you will learn new skills and increase your value in the marketplace for the long term, you may even take less money than you are earning now.

No one can tell you what your walk away number should be, no one but you. And you should know what this number is. Add up your current compensation and write it down in your notebook. Take a moment and write down the number you are hoping for in the offer. Remember, until you have an offer, you have nothing.

Now write a lesser number underneath it. Would you accept the position for that? Would you walk into your boss's office and present your resignation, refuse a counter offer to stay and go to the good-bye party they will throw for you and listen to everyone cry on your shoulder and tell you how much they will miss you, and you go through with it? OK. Good. Now we are getting somewhere.

Write down a number a few thousand dollars less that the company could offer you. You may be frowning as you write it, but budgets are tight, they don't really know what you can do for them yet. Don't forget that lots of people know how to interview very well. Look at the number, would you resign and accept it?

Again, write down a number a few thousand less than the last. Your feelings might be bruised, and you may feel the need to negotiate but if they didn't budge, would you accept it? Do these exercises until you get to the number where you would be perhaps slightly infuriated. "How dare they?" you might ask yourself. "There is no way I would accept that number."

That is your walk away number. It tells you much about yourself and your current situation. It might tell you that you studied the wrong courses in college, prepared yourself for a disappointing career. Disconnect any emotion from it as you look at it; it is just a number. But you now know that if you receive an offer at that level and under, you will refuse it.

This is tremendously important when you are negotiating, and you'll know that if an offer comes in above this number, you will accept it. You have no business negotiating an acceptable offer. To sit down at the negotiation table in the interview process means first this; that you are ready to set fire to the prospect of working with this company. At any time in the negotiation process, the offer could be rescinded, and sometimes it is. So, you get what you want, or you walk away from it.

Now that you know what an acceptable offer is, you know when to negotiate and when not to. If the offer comes in at or under your walk away number, you could state: "Your offer is very interesting to me. I like these aspects of it (name them), however, for me to undertake the increase in responsibilities and walk away from some advancement down the road at my current situation, I would need to see an offer for _____ (state the number)."

If the employer states that this is out of their range and they are not able to do this, point out your strengths once again and give weight to the value that you bring and go silent. If there is nowhere to go, end the interview by showing gratitude and leave the door open for further communication. Sometimes these things come back to life later.

REFERENCE CHECK

At some point in an interview process you will be required to submit references. Most of the time, companies want co-workers and past employers. They want to talk to the higher ups, your supervisor or division leader, people who have knowledge and an opinion on the wake you left behind. Your references should be accomplished and articulate. They should regard you highly and be able to address your strengths and possibly your weaknesses.

The person checking your reference will be cross checking it off their own impression from the interview with you, and will customize their questions to areas of concern that they may have.

Here are some questions that your referees could be asked:

1. What connection do you have with _____ ?

2. How long have you known this person?

3. What period of time did you work with them?

4. How would you compare their results with others in a similar function?

5. What can you tell me about their work history regarding promotions to get him to his current position?

6. How do you perceive their ability to interface with people outside their company?

7. How do you perceive their ability to interface with management in the organization?

8. How many people did they perceive directly?

9. How would you describe their management style?

10. What kind of workload did they take on and how did they handle it?

11. How would you describe their energy level?

12. What are your thoughts on their ability to learn and be creative at solving problems?

13. How would you view their attention to detail?

14. What would you say about their quality of work?

15. Are they more people or technically orientated?

16. To your knowledge, do they have any problems that would compromise their work?

17. In your opinion, what is their major strength?

18. From your experience with them, what areas do you feel need improvement?

19. What is the best way to supervise them?

20. How would you describe their attendance and punctuality on the job?

21. How would you describe their professional presentation?

22. If they were qualified for a position in your company today, would you rehire them?

23. Do you have any additional thoughts you would care to contribute?

You can see that when someone gets a call and is asked these questions, the company checking into your background is going to know what that person's opinion of you is. And that's fine, especially if it's glowing and good.

What will your references say about you? Do you know? Select your referees carefully and provide them with this form, ask them to fill it out and return it to you. This will give you an idea how they will answer. If you like what they wrote, you can even provide this form, filled out by a reference along with the name, to show that you have already done their work for them.

Contact the people who you will ask for your references. Ask them this question: "I would like to use you as a reference. What would you be able to say about me and my work performance? Is there any reason why you may caution me against giving your name as a reference?" Listen to their words carefully. Many people will be honoured to speak on your behalf but others may not feel the same and you should know why.

Make no mistake; a good reference can get you the job you want. It can be the extra push that launches you across the finish line, just ahead of the other candidate, or it can be the straw that breaks the camel's back and eliminates you from the process.

Take a look at the start date that you have in mind. If the interview team should ask you what day you can start, be prepared with a specific date. Know how much vacation you will need. Do you have any vacations scheduled in the near future? You will need to clear this time on the calendar with your new prospective employer.

Are you expecting any other offers? Know which job you want as a priority and know how the others rate. If you are involved in other processes and are unclear about which one you do want, meditate on it and listen to your inner voice. You know it already. It's the opportunity that is making you put off the other offers. It is the one you call back first. It is the one that you schedule immediately and put off the others.

—————— ACTION STEP ——————

Rewrite your résumé again; know every detail with relation to dates and think of another accomplishment you could add. Show it to a friend and ask them to critique it.

CHAPTER 8

DIFFERENT TECHNIQUES

"Whatever games are played with us,
we should play no games with ourselves."
– Ralph Waldo Emerson

The key to interview preparation is to know yourself. If you are well prepared for the interview, you will give them an accurate picture of your skills and ambition level. When preparing for the interview, you should go into the meeting with seven questions that you have written down on a legal pad that will go with you. I recommend the following seven questions:

1. "I was wondering if you could describe the position to me?"

    The risk in asking this question is that you may come across as slightly overbearing, therefore, this must be done with the utmost tact. But the advantage of asking this question is that you will learn what is most vital and get a perception of the level of urgency and pain associated with the position open.

2. "What is the most important thing I should focus on if I get selected and start this position?"

    Listen to the answer and relate your strengths to this vital area. If you have solved these types of problems, or worked with the software that is related to this vital area of the position, state it.

3. "What is the most important qualification you are looking for in the candidate you hire?"

If you are strong in the area he or she mentions, make sure to verbally highlight it again.

4. "If I am selected and I start employment in this position, what will be the biggest challenge I will face?" This is a 'look under the rug' question. With this question you are looking for problems as well as looking to sell yourself as a problem solver.

5. "When you look at my background, do you have any doubts or concerns about my ability to be successful in this position?" This nails it, doesn't it? If he or she relates a concern that is true; for example, it is a strong sales position and you have not done a great deal of selling in your career. Be thankful that it is mentioned now, because you have a chance to address it before you leave the interview.

   So, anticipate this question as you prepare for the interview and try to answer it with something like: "While it is true that I have not had the opportunity to really develop my sales ability, I do feel that I have always had it. I am confident that with the right training and mentoring, I can pick it up fast and be a great asset to the position and help the company reach its goals."

   You should prepare an honest and truthful answer to this question in advance. Practise your answer and develop the ability to communicate it quickly.

6. "How do I stack up against the other candidates you are interviewing?"

   This is a fair question and should be asked near the end of the interview process. This direct question will show the interviewer that you are competent and realistic. There is nothing wrong with pushing the boundaries, the interviewer needs to remember you above other candidates – let it be because you had a good, well thought out question.

There is also a closing question you can ask, if you detect that the opportunity is slipping away from you.

7. "If I don't hear from you by Friday, what should I assume?"

    This question should rest their fears about you being too shy to do so in the field.

Close the interview by summarizing what you have learned about the position and relate these things to your strengths. This will demonstrate that you were listening and help you show your mental agility. Don't worry if you need to ask for clarification on something or if you need to ask for something to be re-clarified. It is best to nail down the carpet where it rolled up before you leave the room, and the summary you give is the chance to do that. Then, at the end of your summary, ask: "Do you have any further questions about my qualifications?"

It is important to flush out any concerns the interviewer may have before you leave the room. Also, if you like what you have heard about the company and are excited about the prospect of receiving an offer, let the interviewer know this. "I believe I have the skills you are looking for and would like to be a part of this team. What is the next step in the process?" you may ask.

I had a candidate say at this point in the interview: "When do I start?" The interview team laughed at his directness and ended up hiring him. People hire people who want to work for them; they are not impressed with coy, smug, self-satisfied people who play hard to get. Smile when you ask this question, a smile is inviting and shows the interviewer that you like them and this will help them like you.

Sometimes it may appear that the interviewer has not prepared questions and simply asks you about something on your résumé. They simply spin questions off of the answer that you provide, drilling down into what you are saying, quietly asking for more information about each of your answers.

It's OK to break the question and answer with a question of your own – it keeps the flow of information from being too one-sided and shows your ability to assert yourself. It also calls the interview to move off topic when enough drill down has been done.

When you get to your home or office, it will be time to break out your interview notebook and write thoughts down for later review. Immediately after the interview you are the last person who should give an opinion of what transpired because you are too close to the situation and need to gain some distance from it.

An interview is a stressful situation and, because the stakes are sometimes high, we can have a reaction dump right afterwards. Write down the questions that are bothering you. Then write the answers that you wish you had stated.

Don't be surprised if you find them trivial or silly later on. You may also find a gem of wisdom that can help in your next interview. The self-review needs to be written down – when stored in the notebook it can be reviewed with objectivity later. Recall questions that you were unprepared for and list them. Write down what your answer was, as best as you can remember and fill up a page of what you wish you had said. This stuff is gold and can be mined later.

When you are invited back for a second interview, make sure that you leverage the experience from your first interview in this meeting. The first interview and the second interview may be connected; if it is with the same people, the threads of the first interview can be picked up and the conversation can be continued to some degree.

Becoming complacent or overfamiliar with the interview team during the second interview is a mistake. The temptation to engage with the interview team with your guard down will be easier; they will be more comfortable with you, some of the members of the interview team may genuinely like you (what's not to like – right?) and hope that you get the job. Although it is good to relax, it keeps you sharp and allows your creative energy to flow. But remember your strategy and maintain a high level of professional presence with critical questions and responses.

So, always make sure that before going into the second interview you review your notes and try to recall the feeling from the first interview. Were there any specific questions they asked that you can expect more of in this meeting? Then there would be no excuse to not be prepared for them.

Guess what some of the interviewer's concerns may have been in the first interview; write a list of questions that you can anticipate in your notebook. This list of anticipated

questions will be a training tool; you can rehearse addressing them several times while attempting to improve your
response each time. Ask the question out loud again and
answer it again, with a different expression on your face,
emphasizing different words, and come at the answer from a
different, more creative angle.

When you feel like you have prepared enough based on the
experience of the first interview, prepare some questions that
you want to ask. Was there something that the interviewer
said which caused you concern about the level of expectation of the role? Here, your notes will be vital for recollecting
concerns. "In our last meeting, I especially enjoyed hearing about the advanced tools that will be available to me. I
wondered about these advancements – how do they affect
the results as far as the team's production? Has the overall
performance been raised upon implementation?"

Formulate your questions with precise verbiage and
rehearse them.

———————— ACTION STEP ————————

Go to your local library and check out every book they have
on interviewing and read it over a weekend. Note ideas that
you want to remember in your *Interview Strategy* notebook.

CHAPTER 9

THE PANEL STYLE INTERVIEW

"When you know that you're capable of dealing with whatever comes, you have the only security the world has to offer."

– Harry Browne

Panel style job interviews are some of the most stressful that a candidate can endure. A panel style interview is anytime you face more than one person in an interview. You should expect the number of people you face to be proportional to the stress factor and complexity of what is transpiring. You may feel that the entire meeting is spinning out of control – questions are just spilling out of you to keep pace with the tempo of waiting questions, as are expectant answers that examine areas of your life that you have not thoroughly studied. The more you want the position or feel that you need the position, the more anxiety you feel. Just when you've recovered your composure, there's another question that has you blathering on about your weaknesses and then trying to explain them and each expression on the faces of the panel is different and telling you something else. So again, preparation is key. We can take action to avoid the worst happening in the interview, then we make specific plans to ensure that it does not go that way. I call it thinking backwards.

Take three paper plates and a thick black marker. You can laugh as you do this, but do it anyway as it will help, I promise. Draw a face on one of the paper plates, go into as much detail as you would like – if you have artistic expression and have been longing to use it, go ahead. Give it hair, glasses, a chin, whatever. The point is this first plate face is friendly, it smiles at you. If you are not artistic, a plain smiley face will do just fine.

Take the next paper plate and draw a stern face instead – this face has a slight frown across the face. The eyes should be drawn, not in circles but perhaps they slant from the nose area up towards the top of the ear, giving them a notorious look of displeasure.

With the third face all the features should be made circular, the mouth a circle, perhaps in surprise, or it might look like it is speaking. The eyes are circular as well, perhaps in inter-est, the point being it could be open to interpretation at the moment – this expression is not static but changing. Then tape the three paper plates to a wall and place a table in front of it. This is your interview panel.

This panel has gathered to make a critical decision about who to hire in a company that desperately needs the right person in this job or it could be mission failure for everyone involved. This panel reports to a board of directors who are fed up with what is going on and have threatened heads to roll and careers to end if there is not a turnaround of results in the next quarter, capeesh?

Sit in front of the three faces, each with a different expres-sion, and read aloud these interview questions, imagining that the first one was coming from the one on the left of you, the smiley face.

"What is wrong with your current position?" the plate face has asked you. Your answer might sound something like:

"There is nothing wrong with my position itself, it is right for someone, but for me it has some limitations with regard to the utilization of my skill sets and positioning for the future. The work itself was challenging when I began it three years ago, but some changes have been implemented that are making me feel that a more productive career move could be out on the horizon for someone with a high level of ambition, such as myself."

Of course, your answer will be uniquely your own, and you may want to answer the question three times before moving on. Take care to maintain a pleasant level of eye contact with all three plates, and keep your back straight and your shoulders pulled back, and yet look relaxed.

From the grouchy plate, the following question will come: "Why should we hire you?" Imagine that the tone of the question is a little terser than it needed to be. Remind yourself not to be offended or put off by questions that get to the heart of the matter. Your answer might sound something like this:

"I appreciate that question more than you may realize as we are here to explore this. I can tell you that my background has been one of success and goal achievement, and I know that this is critical in the industry. The job posting mentioned that you are looking for someone with the qualifications that I have, as well as the number of years of experience in the industry; and I can add, that I have formal training in the specific software that you use."

Now if you feel like you want to spar a bit here, you have laid the groundwork in your answer to be able to ask Mr. Grouchy a question in return. You could add:

"Can you give me a reason why I should want to work here?" Is this too 'in your face' for your personality? Then soften it like this, "What is the best thing about working here?" Look for the sternest interviewer to answer this question. Confront the opponent in the interview early, direct communication with effective questions behind them to show that you are a contender and could win him over to your side.

You taking on Mr. Grouchy may also endear you to the other hiring authorities who wish someone would stand up to him. On the other hand, if Mr. Grouchy is the final say in the process, it depends on the inter politics of what is going on, and there is no way for you to know this so go confidently with your intuition and let the chips fall where they may.

The expression on the centre plate, the one with open eyes and a circular mouth may ask:

"What are your long-term and short-term financial goals?" You may feel that your financial goals are none of their business, but know that it speaks volumes about your intelligence and drive. Position your answer wisely, and be prepared to delve into what you hope to invest in, saving account goals and income goals. Sound like someone who dreams big and has vision, but can build a structure of reality beneath it.

Practice these questions:

- What does the word 'success' mean to you?

- What are your assets / liabilities as a person?

- What would your previous employer say about you?

- Describe your ideal job.

- Does your current employer know you are looking for another job?

- Can you give me an example of when you took instruction well?

- Where have you been successful before? Why?

- What is the biggest challenge in your industry?

- How do you define motivation?

- What were the last five books you read?

Continue answering the questions until you are comfortable addressing multiple faces, keeping eye contact appropriately with each. Review your answers and try it again. Don't hesitate to answer the question, pause and answer it again. Record your answers and listen to the influx and tone of your voice for ways to improve. Repeat answering the question and you will notice the improvement.

The length of your questions needs to be timed. If you are speaking for more than two minutes, it is time to be silent and wait for the next question, with a pleasant look of expectation on your face. If you have combined several points in your answer, when you finish the answer ask: "Did I answer your question?"

Next, imagine that the grumpy paper plate face asks you a question about your previous employer that clearly addresses something dark. He is baiting a trap to get you to speak ill of a former employer. Don't take the bait. It is imperative that you are able to be at peace with companies you have worked for and anyone you have worked with. An invitation to spill the beans is a trap to be avoided. There is no room in life for vengeance, regret or sour grapes. And it certainly doesn't belong in an interview.

Again, it is important to flush out and address any concerns the interviewers may have before you leave the room. So, you need angry face to state what is on his mind. You need him to say what he is thinking while you are in the room, lest he say it after you leave.

Angry face finally lets you know what he is thinking: "You tout yourself as having the experience in the product development area but I know Jack Thompson and he stated you were more the salesman of the team." This is good. Address it directly, just as he did.

The worst thing that he can do is question your background or abilities after you leave the room and spread the shadow of doubt over the interview team when you are not there to address it. By nailing it down before you leave, you remove this threat.

"I do know Mr. Thompson and I enjoyed working with him. I think what he may have meant was that I had a combined role in the project. Initially I was in the development of the idea, but when it was up and running the project manager asked me to go out and sell the design to our clients so that we would have a running platform to step onto when we released it.

"Mr. Thompson may not have known that because by the time he was assigned to the team, I was already out on the road. But much of the design that made that product work was mine. I drew up the plans and communicated the strategy to the team. In fact, I was lead designer for the first six weeks. Since he joined the project after the design work had been completed, I can understand why he would say that by mistake.

"Does that clear up any misunderstanding?" After angry plate answers, follow up with a softener: "I appreciate your bringing that up, I wouldn't want you to think I had falsified anything in my past or my qualifications. That's why in this interview I am attempting to give you the most accurate information about my background that I can." Smile slightly at the angry plate face taped to the wall.

If you are interviewing in a position that is out of your industry, there may be an undercurrent of concern about your ability to transition from one industry into another. If the interview team is touching on it, or dancing around it without addressing it directly, there is an issue here and you should ask this question: "I want to be successful in my next career move, and I am applying for positions that will challenge and stretch my limitations so that I grow into my next role. When you look at my background, do you have any concerns about my ability to morph my pharmaceutical sales background into the business franchise sales industry?"

Flush out their concerns and then nail them down. Imagine the face plates looking at you and responding with their concerns: "Well, now that it's out there, what makes you think you can transition your skills into this industry?" the angry plate face asks you.

"Well, yes, and thank you for that question because it leads me into what I would like to say to you. If you look at my history, I didn't always sell pharmaceuticals, I used to sell cars at Plymouth Ford. And in the summer, during my college years, I worked at the suicide hot line where I literally sold life itself to people who were despondent.

"Life is a continuous transition and I believe that I can sell the business to people because I believe we are all self-employed. I just need to know what support systems you have available to help people as they begin." Look at all the members of the panel.

"Sales are a transfer of enthusiasm. I have that and I can transfer it with my communication skills. Does it really matter what the product is? Once I learn the ins and outs, I will be your top salesman, no matter what we are moving." End with the gentle smile, not too big, just enough to show you are comfortable.

The trick here in this interview strategy is to get the interview team to ask you the right question. I am reminded of a quote from Philip Dormer Stanhope, 4th Earl of Chesterfield: "Never seem wiser or more learned than the company you are with. Treat your learning like a watch and keep it hidden. Do not pull it out to count the hours, but give the time when you are asked."

This is the principle of this technique. Get them to ask you what the biggest concern on their minds is, and then address it directly with a well-prepared response. The disqualification method is used by an interviewer who is trying to weed you out, and would rather not take the time to get to know you, so he simply asks you to do the job for him.

These questions might sound like this:

- What are your weaknesses?

- Why shouldn't I hire you?

- Tell me about your least favourite boss.

- Why have you had so many job changes?

- Does your present employer know that you are looking for another job?

- Everyone has their baggage, what would you say yours is?

- What sorts of people annoy you the most?

- Tell me about the least interesting work you have ever done.

These are some examples of questions that move to your weakness and edge you forward into saying bad things about yourself. As a candidate, you should institute simply never to say anything bad about yourself or admit to your weaknesses. I am suggesting that you keep your mind focused on the ball, and veer your answers towards ways of speaking to your strengths.

"What are your weaknesses?" Angry plate face has demanded of you. You look around the room, as though you are stunned, lost for words. And the only time in an interview you are actually lost for words is when you want to use the effect of it, such as now.

"I just can't think of any right now. But I do know that I am strong in Jack Henry accounting software, and I do know that your organization uses that. Also, I am a Six Sigma Black Belt; did I mention that? As far as weaknesses, I am a positive person and I tend to gear my thinking in a different way and focus on positive traits in myself and others."

Another way of dealing with the question of your weaknesses is to speak to of some obvious but not so crucial facts. "I wonder if you have seen the fact that I live 15 miles from town, this is a weakness for me as far as community interaction goes. But I can tell you why that should not be a concern …"

"Does your current employer know you are looking for another job?"

"Does anyone really know what anyone else knows? I do know that my background in working with the FDIC would be a great asset to the bank in the next audit." It's time for the million dollars smile.

"My least favourite job? Well, nothing directly comes to mind, but I can tell you that it would be the one that had the least challenge. It would have been the one in my past that didn't let me use my above average intelligence to solve problems that others might feel were mundane. I can tell you that I like the challenges in life." Disqualification questions can only be sidestepped. How can you directly answer a question to your weakness and look good? This is not a confessional or a time to bleed to heal your inner wounds.

Ideally, the interview goes like this; you realize that you like this company and that you want the job on offer. Then you must succeed in telling the interviewers how you can do the job well, better than anyone else they are talking to, and tell them what you would like to do in your future and how the company can be a part of that. Then the company comes back to you with the extension of an opportunity that will change your career direction and your life.

——————— ACTION STEP ———————

Identify four companies that you think you might like to work for and research them extensively.

CHAPTER 10

THE OFFER

"Beware the naked man who offers you his shirt."
– Navjot Singh Sidhu

An offer can come in an interview at any time. If you recieve an offer early in the interview process, this indicates you have done several factors right. If the company puts their best foot forward, they impress you with a decent package.

An offer can come:

- At the conclusion of the first interview. If the company is nimble and the person you are speaking to has the authority to do so, and knows how to wield it, yes. Not often, but it can happen.

- At the conclusion of several interviews that sometimes thoroughly test a candidate's patience.

- At a separate ceremony over coffee from an impressive figurehead in the company.

- In the form of an email from a human resource department.

- Through a recruiter or some third-party consultant involved in the hire.

- On the rebound after the first candidate of choice has turned it down because there was not enough vacation time in it, and it had a crappy bonus structure. (So, he would say.)

- In the form of a letter, six weeks since you last heard from anyone at the company and have not had a call returned from them in all that time.

- At a business party from the CEO of your chief competition, after you have finally beaten him at a golf game.

For a moment, envision in your mind the company of your dreams. Envision a company that you are eager to lease your skills to, as CEO of your personal financial corporation. Hear the number, it's huge. You are in a room full of people; the hiring manager stares at you, gauging your reaction to the immaculate extension of lavishness in salary and benefits.

You realize that this is a tremendous opportunity for you to pursue in order to advance in your career. You accept it immediately and nail down a start date. When you are interviewing for a job you know that you want, it's easy to have it go that way. But if you haven't made up your mind that you want to work at this company yet, and they extend an offer to you, the interview process can feel that it's not long enough.

If you haven't yet decided that you want to work for the company, an offer extended to you too early will feel awkward if you are not prepared to field it correctly. You were in selling mode, convincing them that you were the candidate for the job. So you convince them, because you are getting better at this the more you do it, and you get an offer. Now you are in the hot seat and you must ask the questions to get all the details you need to make your decision. Don't succumb to the surprise of having been given the job, even if at that moment you are unsure about wanting it.

"And who is my direct supervisor?" you ask. Collect all the information you may need and write it down. This motion will prepare them for what you are about to do.

"This is a very generous and inviting offer, I just need to look it over. Would it be acceptable for me to respond by the end of tomorrow?"

"Sure, sure, take your time. Think it over. But, let me ask you, which way are you leaning?" smiley plate asks you.

"This is very exciting. I'm not leaning, I'm more like reeling," say, if this is true, and smile. There isn't much more you can do here so leave the room and begin your thinking process with pen in hand.

And let's not forget that the offer can be rescinded at any time and, if you are not tactful and well-spoken, you can negotiate yourself out of a tremendous opportunity. So, it is important that you accept the offer when it is acceptable. Again, you must know your walk away number in advance, this must be held in your mind as you discuss compensation. It's a reference point. A way of seeing in a blackened room because you have a point of reference. In essence, sadly, your walk away number is how much you will allow your next potential employer to value you. If they will not pay you more than what you are making now, why would you go to them? To learn more skills, work on a better team, and advance your employment peer group possibilities.

However, when you decide it is time to make a move, you must recognize your own worth before anyone else will. The process of making changes should be a move forward in many aspects.

Give thought to turning down the opportunity of a lifetime because of the package you are used to. Put dollar value to the benefits you enjoy and want to keep. Prepare to negotiate for them, explain why they are important to you and how, with them, you can perform your duties at a higher level in several ways, and list them. Look at your own financial situation and examine your goals. If the offer comes in below your walk away number, you can say something like:

"Your offer is very inviting but with my current compensation package being what it is, and the changes in my life that I am willing to make to take the position, I would need _____ this number. And if you can meet me there, I can give notice at my job tomorrow and join the organization in two weeks. Please keep in mind my scheduled Canada trip in August." Then smile and look at the decision-maker on the team. Remember to include any vacation that you have scheduled in your statement. It is up to you to transfer that information at this time, to clear it for approval.

The offer is the most significant and the first way that a company will speak to you. It reveals how much they value your past experience, dedication and developed talent. If they come in under your walk away number, you will refuse the offer, without burning bridges or making a show that you were insulted because there is no profit in that. Remember these things can come alive again later.

However, what if you have received the offer but it lacks a week of vacation? When you look over your use of your current vacation, you find that sometimes you don't even use all of your four weeks of vacation, but you would like to think that with your new job you will. Is this worth risking the entire acceptable package for? Think of it this way – let's assume that you are a man. You want to ask a woman to marry you, so you buy a diamond ring and present it to her in a romantic setting. She is clearly thrilled and looks at the ring. But she is dissatisfied with the size of the diamond on the ring. If she were to thrust it back at you and ask for a bigger diamond and a new proposal, this would most likely hurt your feelings and leave you in tatters. But if she accepted and threw her arms around you and kissed you, then said: "By the way, let's get a bigger diamond on the ring, so I can show it to my mother next week." I am almost certain that your reaction would not be as cynical.

Using the same philosophy with the offer being acceptable as it is, accept it first then later ask for the extra week of vacation with some tactful, prepared statements. "Mr. Hiring Authority, I am delighted with the offer and I eagerly accept it. My start date can be 13 October. Just let me know what time and where to report, but incidentally, I do have a request. The three weeks' vacation as a part of the package is one week less than I am getting now, and I do have some family plans coming up that require me to attend certain functions in the summer. It's no deal breaker, but is it possible that I could receive four weeks' vacation when I start?"

It never hurts to ask. But realize it is a request and not a demand. You are now asking for something as an employee, as opposed to a potential recruit. It may have more weight or it may not, but if you want the job and the offer is acceptable, make sure you secure it fast.

What if you have been interviewing but no offers are coming? Then it is time to debrief your interview notebook. Write down the name of the company, who you met with and the time and date of the interview. Answer the following questions routinely:

- How long was the interview? What specific questions stand out in your mind? Did they describe the position to you? Did you feel that the position played to your strengths?

- Was there any tension in the interview? What was the source? Was there a specific question that ended the interview? Write it down.

- Do you want the job? Why?

- What will you do next time? In what way were you unprepared? What do you feel went well?

- How did it end? What follow up is required on your part?

- How did this position fit into your career development plan?

- How long did you spend preparing for the interview?

Make this questionnaire a template that you fill out each time you are interviewed. Before each interview, review this notebook and look over your last three interviews – this will help you prepare for the experience and bring forward the lessons that you need to sharpen up before you step into the process again.

This notebook will be a valuable tool when preparing for other interviews. In review, you will gain insight into what type of positions you are finding yourself attracted and responding to. You may also observe patterns with the types of questions you are fielding well and not so well. You will also gain insight into your own mind, and begin to get an idea of how the job market is responding to you and you to it. You should be ready to accept your findings without being too hard on yourself.

——————————— ACTION STEP ———————————

If you are working in a work place right now and it has a cube, or a desk, or a work station of some sort that you are assigned to use daily, look at it for a moment. Count each personal object that you have there and see it as a way of you vesting yourself here, in the place and deciding to stay. Bear in mind this quote from Heraclitus: "Everything flows. Nothing stays."

CHAPTER 11

IT'S A GAME — PLAY IT

"Only the prepared speaker deserves to be confident."
–Dale Carnegie

Interviewing and considering your suitable career options is a game. If that sounds like a trite statement, remember that everything is a game in some way. Beginning with the end in mind, it's important to take some time and consider the resignation part of the process.

Let's say you get an offer for an exciting job. You use your decision-making process to select this option because it feels right, looks right and is a move forward in your career. You accept the offer. Now it is time to resign from your current post. This may be an exciting time. You may relish it in anticipation, especially if you have not enjoyed employment with your current company. This will be easy, you think. On the other hand, you may be ready to leave but may be apprehensive about resigning, if you have genuinely enjoyed your current position, and are hopeful that they will understand. What both situations have in common is that the resignation may not go as planned, but can become a major, professional ordeal. In fact, you may be walking into the most professionally dangerous meeting of your career. Be prepared.

With the rising cost of training a new employee, losing a valuable member of the team can be very costly for a company. Also, some managers take it personally when someone leaves. It reflects upon the retention skills of the management team and losing certain people can frankly be devastating for a company.

If you think your current employer is just going to let you walk out the door with all your knowledge of the company and relationships with clients and jump right into the arms of another organization, particularly if it is a competitor, you could be mistaken. The boss who never really had much time to talk to you, showed you no appreciation, but yet still you admired if for no other reason than he was your boss, will suddenly take an interest in you when he receives your resignation letter. Imagine him now glancing up at you over his glasses with concern as he reads your resignation letter. "John, what a surprise, I am not ready for this. Please, shut the door, sit down and let's talk."

In your mind, suddenly you are questioning your resolve because, after all, it is comfortable here, they like you and know what is expected of you. You think of the option at the other company and it seems frightening and the challenge that it offers does not feel so attractive to you. The lure of comfort has begun to wind around you like a boa constrictor as you sit in the leather chair from where you consider change. The pit of your stomach has formed into a knot of tension and the confliction that you feel there dissipates temporarily as you consider taking back your resignation. What were you thinking anyway? These people are fantastic and there is no need to go through the stress of a job change when these guys are really great.

If you have not prepared for such a conversation and your motivation for leaving has not been well examined by you beforehand, you could fall prey to the counter offer. If you accept the counter offer and retract your acceptance, it is likely that you will regret this decision later. From my experience, 70% of people taking this course of action go on to regret staying and find that the original reasons they had for leaving persist.

Know that if you stay, you may be remembered as the person who had to be bought to remain on the team. Your loyalty will be in question and you may find yourself outside the inner circle. You may experience fewer invitations into select meetings. They may begin to see you as someone who is on their way out. Now that you no longer fit, they will be looking to replace you with someone who is more of a team player.

The answer is that once you accept an offer, make a commitment to resign. See it as already done and don't allow your mind to rethink it. But if you have no intention of leaving, don't play the game of faking a walk to the door. Either stay or go, but do not gamble with your current employer. Remember what you are trying to achieve and fix your eye on the horizon.

Let's sit in front of the face plates on the wall and practise. Hold your hand up, showing the palm and drop your eyes to stare momentarily at the floor. "Please don't make this any harder than it has to be, my decision is final." Now raise your eyes and look at the hiring authority. This would not be a time for a smile but instead a conciliatory expression with palms perhaps tipped upward, showing.

"Is this about money?" the face plate with the kind expression asks, testing your resolve with compensation, a company's most powerful tool. Think of this, anything they needed to do to keep you, should have been done by now. You just resigned; you cannot un-ring a bell that you have just rung.

"No, not at this point, it's about my future and I see it someplace else from here on. Do you need my two weeks?" Wrap it up so you can get out of there, but try not to burn bridges.

"The president of the company is having lunch with me in half an hour. We are going to a restaurant, why don't you join us and allow us to talk to you about this."

"I appreciate the offer, but I have some things to wrap up here and I don't see the point in joining you. Unless this is about goodbye, in which case I would love to attend. Will you require me to stay the two weeks?" Try tactfully to get him to release you from this obligation so that you can be on your way. Some people have said that the worst two weeks on a job were the ones after they resigned. You can sometimes expect the worst assignments, be seen as a threat to the motivation of other staff and seen as though you have already left. It can be creepy and you feel like a leper.

And worse, you, yourself may feel that you are already gone as well. What's the point? Your mind is transitioning to your new job. Your life is on hold for this time but commitment to your end result of establishing separation from your current employer must be achieved, as this is your exit strategy.

Despite the length of the interview process, you should always prepare yourself for the resignation stage. And to finish the race, sometimes you must endure a long, drawn out hiring process that can prove to be tedious and overbearing. So play the game, enjoy it and learn everything you can from it. Keep notes in your notebook on the people you meet and the interview questions you are asked. All of this adds to your master plan to become an expert level interviewer.

End every interview by asking what the next step is in the process and nail down a commitment when you can. If you are told that you will be contacted next week, as you leave the office, hesitate with your hand on the door knob. "What should I assume if I don't hear from you by next Friday?" Make eye contact and smile slightly. It is hard to be angry with someone who wears a friendly smile well. If you are not contacted as promised, do not become distraught or disappointed, simply call the person you last met with, if you get a voice mail, leave a friendly, upbeat message like this:

"Hi Don, this is Terry Franklin. I met with you last Wednesday regarding the Chief Financial Officer position. I thought we had a very nice conversation and I am interested in moving forward. You had mentioned that I would get a call by yesterday afternoon and because I haven't heard from you, I thought I would call to follow up. My number is _____. I look forward to hearing from you."

Track the process you have going on. This will assist you in being able to perform an impressive follow up, meaning a call, email or letter to the hiring manger to inform them you appreciated the conversation and are enquiring as to the next step in the process.

Candidates who follow through will more often move forward in the process and be remembered more favourably. It's your email they find when searching in backtrack mode for candidates, because you sent it. Many did not. Good follow up is the trademark of a competent professional who remembers conversations, people's names and tough questions. When you remember things about people, it shows that you care about them and are a good listener. It is an effective skill to be able to pick up a conversation from two weeks ago and complete it like it was an hour ago. Organize your interviews, store the information and review it frequently.

These types of thoughts will position you in life with people of like mind who can help you reach your goals. Many successful people are skilled at positioning themselves in this world, and it can start with the interview. Think about what your position is in your current employment situation? How have you positioned yourself with available opportunities? Consider where you are now. Ask yourself these questions and write down your answers:

- Who is next in line for promotion in the company?

- Have I been passed over for promotion in the last five years and why?

- Is this a company that has an impenetrable upper management tier?

- Who is ahead of me in the line of succession for promotion?

- What is my future here with this company?

Many managers are good at placation and appeasing discontentment with kind words when an employee asks for a raise. Learn to see through such words and analyse the actions of your current employer. Any promotion that does not come with increased income or real earning potential is not advancement in your career. It is a sign you are being taken advantage of.

A realistic evaluation of your current employment situation and others you have had in the past will help you to recognize future potential opportunities. You will be able to evaluate and increase your skills for potential future employment positions. You will be building a template of what a good opportunity looks like and what you will need to be suitable for it. The better you get at it, the more effective you will become at asking the right questions to hiring managers and uncovering opportunities. In the interview process you can ask questions about positioning that will reveal what the framework for advancement may be in the near future.

You might ask in the interview:

"What sort of promotional opportunities are available for someone who performs well?"

"As you look down the road, are there any retirements approaching that will open up advancement for members on the team that I am applying with? What are they?"
Learning how to examine positioning in an organization can give you the edge to recognizing real future potential in a company structure.

If you come across too much like a hotshot that will not be happy in the role they are considering you for, this line of questioning could weigh against you. Balance your enquiries with temperament and tact. Good companies frequently prefer to promote from within.

"Does this organization have a history of promoting from within?" you may ask. Listen for stories, examples and future growth that will highlight a bright future for you. Ask the hiring manager how he came to work here at the company and listen for a promotion story.

After completing an interview, make your afterthought notes and describe the positioning of the role you are interviewing for. Is it better than the one you are in? Is it a move forward in your career or backwards? Is this vital to you? Five years from now, if you stay at your current employer, will you be better off with the perspective organization? List the reasons why.

Are you interviewing with a company that has a bunch of grey-haired geezers running it who are about to retire? If so, are they thinking of training in the next realm of management and executive level power brokers, or will they sell this company to the highest bidder by the end of the year?

If that should happen, what would a purchasing company think of your skills? Would they see you as a real value or replace you with their own team?

——————— ACTION STEP ———————

1. Write your resignation letter and keep it in your planner. Begin it, "Dear Client,"

2. Keep a bag in your desk drawer for your exit.

3. In your notebook, make a prediction: if a competing company purchased the one I currently work for, would they keep me and promote me? Would they fire me because my counterpart in their organization already has more of the market share? Let it sit overnight and read it tomorrow after you sleep on it.

CHAPTER 12

YOUR PERSPECTIVE FROM 10,000 FEET

*"Within you there is a stillness and
a sanctuary to which you can retreat
at any time and be yourself."*
– Hermann Hesse

Opportunities abound around you, and there has never been a better time to be capable, talented and skilled. By being successful, you will be able to make more competent business decisions on a large scale that will impact more people. With a history of success in your business dealings you can give more of your money to charity and assist other people who are in need. With more resources, you will be able to provide more help to your family members and be more generous in times of need.

Having a vision isn't something that you read from a mission statement – it's something that fuels you. And when a prospective employer begins to examine your intellect and motivation, know that he will find it. Be ready to describe the things that you want, that you think about. A person who wants something is ten times stronger than a person who wants nothing. If you are competent, reliable and can achieve results, you should not sell yourself short. The world truly is your oyster and if you have ambition and a dream, you can make it happen. So, when constructing your dream, observe the lay of the terrain for a moment and look at geography.

Are you living in the place you would like to be in? Can you relocate to achieve your goals? If you could live anywhere you wanted to, where would you like to be? Where are your family and friends right now? If you have children, how old are they and is this the community you would like them to be raised in? Are they old enough to leave the house and are you and your spouse an empty nest couple, freeing up your geography? Have you had a conversation with your spouse about where you would like to be? If you do move, and you own a house, how would this affect you? These are questions that you should think about and review, then revisit the answers some time later.

If you decide that relocation is an option and is desired, there are things you need to think about and prepare for in the way of career advancement and employment achievement. Do a cost of living comparison on the cities you consider suitable. Compare it and add it to your cost of living estimated expense. This may cause you to raise your walk away number if any position requires this relocation.

A relocation option expands the range of possibilities for your future. Are there certain sectors of the industry booming in any given area of attraction in country or out? Studying these factors will require more research time but it is time well spent.

When applying for a job where you will need to relocate, remember to convince the interviewer that you are taking this very seriously. Despite having no connections to the area, you want the job very much, so much so that you are willing to move to an area that you do not know anyone in, and parachute into this community and wring success out of the plan.

The interviewer will study your background looking for how active you are in the community. This is a direct reflection of how outgoing and transferable you are and your ability to adapt and thrive in a new environment, rather than just survive. By pointing out your community involvement you can talk about how it has helped you make new contacts and build your network.

Give a plan for each family member, mention how you have done some research about the area and activities you see yourself getting involved in.

ACTION STEP

Have a conversation with a friend about change. Speak of the importance of being able to roll with change and what courage is required to face it. Speak in favour of it, especially if you never have.

CHAPTER 13

LISTENING TO QUESTIONS

"If you are going to spend all this time fishing,
don't you think you should sharpen your hooks
just in case a fish bites?"
— Don Brose

Tactical skills are required for good interview strategy. If the strategy is a full-frontal assault, the tactics are fixed bayonets. The finest of your tools come together and guide you in conducting yourself in a desirable and intelligent manner during a business meeting and, even more so, in an interview.

Listening is a foundational skill in interviewing — never interrupting anyone — and tact. Tact is defined as: A keen sense of what to say or do to avoid giving offense; skill in dealing with delicate situations. Any situation can be a delicate situation so let's take a look at some techniques of communication that will allow you to probe into a potentially sensitive area of the company.

One of them is front-loading. When I front-load a question, I add a softener before I get to the question. This technique is effective in preventing your question from being taken in a different context than meant. It allows you to control the perception of the question, with a softener for paving the direction.

You want to know: "What happened to the predecessor in this position?" You think about asking this question but think again and then try: "Why is this position open?" Disguise the fact that you are probing for dysfunction in the company.

Try the frontloaded question: "I was looking at the financials posted on the bank; there has been impressive growth in the mortgage lending area. It's a great time to grow. Is this position open from internal growth or did someone leave?" This softener may not only answer the question but harvest more information about the company directly from someone who knows.

You want to ask: "Why is the turnover so high here at this company?" But blurting that question out could cause an ulcer to flare up in one of the interview team members and won't move you closer to the goal, which is to determine what the opportunity level here is with this company and if it is a fit for you.

The front-loaded question you should ask is: "In these challenging times of hiring people who seem unfocused, do you find the work ethic and employee retention the same as it was, perhaps ten years ago?" This will allow the hiring manager to go into his troubles of keeping good people and will allow you a doorway to examine the company's internal core to see what values are being instilled.

In a situation where the position has a sales element to it, or some derivative of performance attached to it, you may want to know how long you have to reach your goal before you are fired. This is understandable. You could be stepping out of your comfort zone when taking on this new position and you are realizing that it will take more time to learn this new field. You are unsure of the competition level within the company, as well as externally, that could affect your performance. You know yourself to be a quick study but challenging positions are called that for a reason. You want a challenge, yet you want the odds of success to be in your favour.

You want to ask: "How long do I have, after I start, before I get fired if I don't perform up to the required standard?" But that question would belie your concern that you may not have the confidence they are looking for. To get a complete answer, use a front-loaded question like: "This position has some elements to it that really excite me as far as using my sales experience and training are concerned. To do this effectively I'll need to establish some new relationships in an industry where currently I have limited contact. Is there a time frame of accountability that I need to be aware of as I approach scheduled reviews, and if someone is struggling, do you have a contingent plan for assistance?" This question should address your concern and give you the feedback you need to know how much slack is in line as you take on a new career and commit all of your resources to this move.

Let's say there is a new CEO of the company, the previous one left in scandal or under questionable terms. You would like to know the philosophy of new management. You want to ask: "What is the CEO like?" But that doesn't quite have the ring to it that you want. The front-loaded question you should ask is: "Leadership is so vital in steering the vessel. I noticed there is a new CEO at the helm. Is there a significant difference in philosophy and direction of the organization with the new command?" This question is vague enough to get the hiring manager talking to you. The interviewer must be comfortable with you to be able to do that.

Good, well-placed questions to the interviewer will also get them to communicate with you, and this will leave a favourable memory of the meeting with mutual communication remembered. When people feel comfortable they feel more at ease to express themselves to people who take a genuine interest.

If you want to know the strictness of the work culture, such as, if your child needs to be picked up after school and you are unable to find someone to do this, you may want to ask: "Can I leave to go pick up my kid during a work day?"

That would be unadvisable. The front-loaded question might sound like this: "I enjoy being a top performer in the positions that I have had. I think an important point in getting the work done in top form is that it is done with the best use of time. If I need to pick up my son from school – and I have my time in and my duties performed above standard – is there an issue with me handling a personal issue during the work day?" Let's put it out there. If it is on your mind, there is nothing taboo or nothing that should not be addressed in an interview.

If this is a concern, bring it up now and give everyone a chance to vent on this issue. If you get a hardnosed response from an old-fashioned management team that would be uptight about someone messing with the work schedule, regardless of that person's performance, you may want to know now.

Carefully list out hot issues like this that need to be covered in an interview and then work out a front-loaded way to express the question. Sit in front of your face plate panel and practise asking the questions that give you concern with a casual and relaxed manner. These are the questions that most candidates do not ask because they are afraid of the answers. For any question that is a concern for you, you must get an answer. You will be making an important decision and the information you gather at this point is vital to your ability to frame the decision. If there is an elephant in the room, speak of it. Speak to it.

What if they don't give you the job because you asked the wrong question? That does not happen if it is worded right. The alternative is to take a job and hope for the best about sensitive issues that are imperative to your ability to immerse yourself in the work culture. Hope is not a strategy.

It helps to have short stories ready to share that are action packed and make you look good. The stories you have to tell are underlining your work ethic (if they are true), they involve you working late, making big commitments and keeping them, getting the job done at any cost, sometimes in the last minute and handling situations well.

The trick to using these stories is that your brag factor is not centre stage in the story but a peripheral fact and not the major focus of the subject. "While working late ..." Or "Being called in to deal with a difficult situation I found." These stories need to be written out so they can be remembered; they can be modified to fit almost any question if you have them clearly defined in your mind. Being prepared for the interview-based question means displaying the fact that you think well on your feet.

───────────── **ACTION STEP** ─────────────

Join a community group or business association networking group and become active. Attend a meeting a month and take on one responsibility at the meeting. Exceed in doing what is asked of you.

───────────────────────────────

CHAPTER 14

QUESTION YOUR OWN JUDGMENT

"It isn't what we don't know that gives us trouble,
it's what we know that ain't so."
– Will Rogers

Interrupt your own thoughts while going through an interview process by devising a way to question your own judgment. This is because the decisions made while going through an interview process are vital and often they need to be checked against our own emotional surge. Examining opportunities can be compared with picking up an object for study. We turn it over, look at it from other angles, in a different light, project its future and estimate its value.

All information gathered needs to be looked at and weighed for value and accuracy. Too often we want something to be true and then charge forward assuming it is. Resist the tendency to underestimate information that is not readily available.

In the *Interview Strategy* notebook that you have created, it is time to construct a fault tree. A fault tree is a problem stated on a diagram (yes, it can look like a tree), the causes of the problem are stated at the top of the tree. The trunk can be constructed of issues related to the problem or individual causes of the problem. Whatever, get the problem in the shape of a trunk and top. The branches that come off the trunk are possible solutions and benefits. Brainstorm every single cause of a potential issue with this career move, leave nothing forgotten.

The most important part of using a fault tree or some other named visual writing exercise to guide your thinking, is that the problem stated is accurate, relevant and of top concern in the perspective career or job change. When you have exhausted all of your concerns you can see them, clearly laid out before you. Step away from the drawing for a moment. When you revisit the drawing, try to see it objectively and develop a feeling for the whole picture. Then look critically at the concerns, and evaluate them more realistically. Next start writing answers that come up and develop solutions to these problems until you've answered each problem with three possible solutions. Evaluate the outcome again with the proper weight of your skills and past performance and ask yourself if your apprehension has subsided.

With this exercise, we seek clarity. When clear on objectives, it transfers into an undercurrent of confidence that shines under the surface of everything you say. When a candidate seems unsure of who they are or what they want, that obscurity is transferred to the interview team.

The confidence you project in an interview will make you appear as a desirable candidate – this will come from your ability to frame decisions, sell your ability, evaluate duties and responsibilities and convey your skills in these areas. It comes from your knowledge of yourself and your industry and knowing where you might fit in.

With every interview and reflection you become more self-aware and confident. Having bounced yourself off of others in a professional setting, you complete an important contest that is vital to your career development. We are alive to develop. We need to thrive and find challenges around us; the profession that you are in right now is an arena and it summons you to challenge on a daily basis.

By becoming clear about what you want, you will project this self-knowledge in an interview and create an impression of strength. This will draw the people who are interviewing you to feel that they should have you on their team.

—————————————— ACTION STEP ——————————————

Join Toastmasters and attend meetings regularly. This will help you gain confidence and poise. Aside from improving your communications skills, it is a great networking group.

CHAPTER 15

GOAL SETTING

"Chance favours those in motion."
– James H. Austin

Your interview notebook should have a section for goal setting. Let's choose five goals to visit daily. One of these goals should be a career goal. You could write: "I will achieve professional satisfaction in an employed capacity with an intelligent company and earn 100,000 dollars a year, while learning new skills. I'll achieve this by _____." and write a date. Underneath this statement write three things (under A, B and C) that you could do to help you achieve this goal.

One of the things that you could write down to achieve this goal is to have a certain number of interviews in a month. How many interviews should you set as a goal? That's your call. It could be one interview a quarter, or three months, which is the minimum if you want to impact your career in any way.

If you want to step up and focus some energy into accelerating your career, you could schedule as many as four in a month. If you live in a populated area that has more opportunities, you could schedule two a week, making a total of eight interviews in a month. But, what if there aren't that many positions being advertised? How could you generate interest in your credentials to companies that are not advertising their needs right now? You could market your skills to the community like any other organization that wants to get the word out on an available product.

Generate a list of companies within a 50-mile radius of where you live and obtain their phone numbers. This is your market list. The more information you can gather and keep in the list, like the name of the President, or the Director of Human Resources, the better for your objective. Next write up a brief marketing pitch about your background that will include your work experience, years of industry production, outstanding achievements and other details that will fit into an elevator pitch of no longer than about 30 seconds.

Then start making phone calls. Ask for the President of the organization – start at the top and when that person gets on the phone, announce who you are with confidence and roll into your elevator speech. End it by asking the question: "Would you be interested in scheduling a time when I can stop at your office and discuss my qualifications in greater detail and discuss employment options with your company?" What industry executive would not want to talk to a player in their space, and especially a shaker and producer such as you?

Be prepared for rejection by being polite, offer to email them your résumé in case they change their mind, and remember to ask for that email address. Shake off any rejection and go on to the next company on your list. Marketing yourself this way will increase your exposure and multiply the number of interviews that you get.

Don't forget to look at sister industries. In other words, if you are an accountant or controller, could you be an accountant or controller in another industry?

Keep track of the feedback you receive, and track and schedule your follow up efforts. Rate the opportunities and rank the desirability of a company and position against each one you look at and the current one. Then rank each opportunity with a consistent scale that weighs as follows:

1.   Compensation; five points total

2.   Nearness to home or desired location; five points total

3.   Forward potential; six points total

Give each option a score in the ranking and then revisit your rate selection.

Visit the goal section of your notebook daily. Write the goals out fresh each day in the morning and read them at night before you go to bed. This will keep your ambition level high and your focus on what is important to you. Moving towards your goal will give you a tremendous feeling of satisfaction and delight, a special feeling that can only come from achievement.

But not all of the experiences in this process are positive. A candidate who is active in interview processes at an enhanced level must be prepared to deal with rejection. Rejection is a fact of life and the more you put yourself out there, and place yourself in selling situations, the more rejection you are likely to receive. When you are rejected, avoid taking it personally. In fact, train yourself to distance your emotions from the response and process it as data to be registered and analysed. A good interview strategy requires that we discipline our disappointments.

When a company informs you that you will not be moving forward in the interview process and are extracted, thank the deliverer of the message for letting you know, and then calmly ask why: "What was the knockout factor?" you could ask. In general, when this notification is given after the interview, it is delivered by someone in human resources that may not have the power to reverse this decision. On the other hand, if you can get feedback directly from the decision maker, you could better explain why you are qualified and push for another meeting to cover this concern. Here are some common reasons for being passed over:

1. You are too old. Yeah, it's a tough world and sometimes that is the case. No sense crying about it. And think about it, if the position is replacing someone who is retiring from the company, do they really want someone who will retire in two years and have to face this again? Of course not. And don't complain about being discriminated against; the entire process is a system of elimination of unqualified candidates. Just move on to a company that won't care how old you are. There are situations where your age won't matter.

2. You are too young. Sometimes more experience is needed, the culture has a certain feel to it and as a kid who is wet behind the ears you don't fit in, and maybe they have enough young punks on the team.

3. You are overqualified. It can happen. They may have a good mentor who wants to school someone in the system and bring them along their way. They may want to groom someone into their culture and not have to retrain the thinking of someone from a big company.

4. You are underqualified. This is something you need to pay attention to. This is where you can learn if there is a skill you are lacking in your industry that it is looking

for. Any rejection for this reason is your own fault and needs to be addressed by you. It's an indication you have been slacking off in training yourself for your profession. Get busy.

5. Your personality was not a match for the team. This means they didn't like you. You may have come across as crass in the interview, or they asked you one question and you answered another; this disconnect made them think you weren't listening or on another plain – have you ever had a conversation like this with someone? It might have meant you weren't listening or you interrupted the hiring authority.

6. You didn't give them enough reasons to hire you. An interview is a chance to wow the hiring authority; sometimes you get just one chance to stand out from a crowd of candidates. You blew it. No one to blame but yourself. Learn from it and move on.

7. You were too late. A hiring team starts to lock in on a candidate and they can fall in love with him or her. After that happens, the rest of the interviews that take place are a mere formality. You couldn't unseat the favourite candidate. Was there a feeling of it being already over before it began in the meeting?

8. You bring too much baggage. They were starting to zero in on you and then you needed so much money, or relocation, or other issues that came up in the process. Maybe you came across like a prima donna that was going to need a bunch of hand holding – who has time for that? Next!

9. Too many moves in your past. This made the company interview team feel like you were on your way someplace else and they might be the next step in your journey, after, of course, they spent a great deal of time training you and investing money in your education for the position. Here you failed to communicate your sincerity in commitment to the position and location.

10. Technical reasons. A particular skill that was required, you were late for the interview, didn't wear a suit, couldn't work Saturdays or the hours didn't fit your special schedule.

It may or may not be a reason from this list, but whatever it is try to find out and don't be discouraged. It will be harder when you really wanted the position and felt like you were right for it. It's tough out there and we all need to steel ourselves for rejection. The last thing you want to do is let it bring you down. Remember this quote from the Roman Emperor Marcus Aurelius: "The first thing is to keep an untroubled sprit. The second is to look things in the face and know them for what they are."

Keep in mind that the experiences and lessons that are gained from these business meetings are very important and life changing. By becoming skilled in the most personal type of business conversation you can have, one that sells your potential and skills, a new depth of communication can be mastered. You can develop a new level of concentration that will increase your listening skills, expand your verbal comprehension and train your mind to follow fast-moving dialogue with highly intelligent people who are shaping the future. When you expand your network with people in your industry, people may remember you later and reach out to you later regarding other options.

The skills that you learn in interviewing will have a tremendous effect on your life skills with your personal relationships. By seeking first to understand people and situations, you will determine methods of interaction that will be more meaningful and enriched. Projecting into the future and making choices each day that will pay off a dividend down the road is how we create our own destiny. Focusing on our future and thinking about how we can benefit in it can be a way of controlling our mind and replacing a destructive way of thinking.

So, keep the long view in mind. Even a year of no job offers is only that; it does not mean that next year will mean the same. Everything changes; you, the industry, the financial climate, the number of people in your industry. All of these things can move just a few degrees and create around you a new world of options that you never dreamed about. And it can happen in a moment, any moment, but the only way you will know it is if you are in motion, rolling the dice.

Remember that you are self-employed. As your own CEO, training and development fall under your list of things to regard. Keep examining the situation and what it is that may be standing in the way of propelling you forward towards your goal. Ask yourself: "What skills must I learn to have the type of job I really want and the offer that I am looking for?" Does this question seem obvious to you? I would challenge you that we should continually drill such questions into our minds and re-adjust our efforts.

Now, in the goal setting section of your notebook, let's write out a scenario where a hiring authority (the angry face plate) has just asked you: "In what ways have you continued your education in our industry, at your own expense?"

"I attend the community college at night and take a Lotus Notes class. To work on my people skills I have been volunteering at the soup kitchen.

"I have been having conversations with my brother about investments. I read two books a month on our industry and subscribe to a publication that updates me with articles on the latest technological developments. This has helped me kindle my passion for what I do."

——————— ACTION STEP ———————

1. Identify any negative or defeatist thoughts that you may have. Remove them from your thinking. Replace them with thoughts of your goals – visualize your end objective.

2. Write out a projection five years into the future.

3. Redo your résumé.

CHAPTER 16

FACE PLATE DRILLS

"The man who comes up with a means of doing or producing almost anything better, faster or more economically has his future and his fortune at his fingertips."
– John Paul Getty

"How did you pay for college?" one of them asks. You answer.

"Was that a competitive environment that you worked in at Coca Cola?"

"Who was the leader in production on the team?"

"Can you tell me a time when you experienced failure?"

"How do you spend your weekday evenings?"

There is a common theme running through this type of questioning. If the questions in this regard came from one of the interview panel, the interviewer is wondering about your motivation. Within your motivation are your work ethics and your ability to concentrate single-mindedly on one thing until it is done.

Motivation is the desire to do things, to stay in motion, to push oneself. Someone who is motivated will have answers that reveal their motivation, they will speak of projects they are taking on at home, study courses they are working on in the evenings, express interest in competitive sports or events of some kind. They will have passions and work to pursue them.

If you are receiving more than two or three questions that are related to your motivation, there could be a doubt here, which should be addressed. Be thankful and nail the answer. To be prepared for questions on motivation, you must know yourself. In your notepad, write down;

- What you really want out of life ...

- What really annoys you ...

- Things that are important to you ...

You may be asked: "Do office give-aways like trips for the top producer entice you?" And you should answer: "Not really. My need to succeed is deeper than that. Don't get me wrong. I will take the trip to Atlantis and enjoy myself, but it is more of a perk of my performance. You see, I always push myself to be the best. I like to have the respect of my peers and I don't like to be number two in anything. I believe in fair competition because it brings out the best in us all, and there are winners and losers in this world, and that's OK, as long as I am not one of the losers." The interviewer wants to see your motivation; give it to them straight.

Another question may be: "What are your goals and how do you plan to achieve them?"

To show the interviewer that you have thought out your future and are activating plans to make this happen, you should answer: "Well, I can share with you the top three from this morning. I want to earn X number of dollars and receive an award for performance in my career this year. I also want to complete a screenplay I am writing and submit it to a contest to see if I can win. I plan on running the Tough Mudder in the spring and I have started training last week. I ran three miles last night after supper and my legs are sore. I could go on, but those are the top three that come to my mind."

Another question that is commonly asked is: "Do you find yourself motivated by money?"

"I think we all want more money, but to say that it is a source of my motivation would not be entirely accurate. It's my belief that people who carry their own engine within them will perform the best they can, whether they are making good money to do it or not. A motivated person who earns a minimum wage will be outworking the people around them simply because that is the way they do it. Sure, we all like to get paid for our work the most that we can, but money to me is really more related to goal-setting than to task reward. Did I answer the question clearly?"

Motivation will be tied to your passions. Someone who genuinely feels a high level of compassion for the poor will gladly spend their Christmas serving food in a soup kitchen to the homeless, and will do it with a joyous heart. These people are truly motivated. In what ways do you display motivation in your life?

Now let's delve into some questions on your personal motivation about career and job change. If the interview team likes you and regards you highly, they will begin to test your portability. They will want to know how likely it is that you will jump from your current employer and accept an offer from them.

These are different types of motivation questions. This motivation is related to your ability to move on from where you are. With these questions they are trying to weed out the tire kickers and vector in on someone who is serious about change.

You need to know what is inside you before they spill it out in the meeting. So, in your notepad write the answer to these questions:

1.   Why leave your current employer now?

2.   When was the last time you received a raise?

3.   What does this position have that your current position does not have?

4.   Are you ready for a change in your career?

5.   Have you talked to your spouse about this or to close friends? What will they say?

6.   What will be the biggest obstacle in your exit strategy from your current employer?

7.   Is there anything in your personal or professional life going on right now that would prevent you from accepting an offer from this company?

8.   Do you want the job?

If there is a burr in your saddle or any incongruity in your answers as they crawl around in your head, the interviewer will feel it. When your motivation for change is being tested and it is in line with your reality, the truth in your answers will have a ring to it that will draw them towards you. If there is any inconsistency, they will feel that as well and under the surface they will be uncomfortable with you.

If there is a lingering question it will present itself after you leave the room. They will turn to each other and say: "He is a good candidate. I like the skills and his personality, but something makes me think he is going to stay where he is."

This is why you must flush out concerns at the conclusion of the interview by asking: "Are there any questions I can answer before I leave, or any concerns that might be on your mind?"And smile slightly. A smile shows you are having fun and, guess what, keep smiling and you will be!

If you should be considering a relocation there are some questions you should be prepared for: "Do you own your home?" If you own a house and need to sell it before you leave, they will feel this out. If so, be prepared with data to show the interviewer that you have a plan to deal with selling or renting out the home.

Be ready with a family plan if you have kids. What will your wife do when you are starting? This is information they will want to know. So show them you have thought it through. This is where you can impress a panel by showing that you have put thought into the details, they will get the impression you are serious.

If you are moving to a new city, get ready to display how you have researched the community, looked at apartments or houses, found a church and plan on joining the Rotary Club that meets in the International House of Pancakes on Thursday morning.

ACTION STEP

Review the last three moves on your résumé and write a paragraph about why you left each place. Don't forget to add what you learned and from whom. Also address the challenges you experienced and be prepared to discuss them.

CHAPTER 17

GRATITUDE

"High levels of perceptual speed are the product of learning, not inheritance."
– Bruce Lee

To prepare for the next technique, let's take out the *Interview Strategy* notebook, and make a list of all your skills, job related or not. Fill a page with activities or skills that you have acquired that have led you to excel in your profession. Put a star by the ones that are job related and let's focus on those.

Beneath each skill, write the names of the people who have taught it to you. Now after each name, write down how they were good at relating the skill to you. Write in as much detail as you can, whether it was their patience, understanding, firm tone – whatever it took to impart that to you, write it down.

When doing this exercise you will find that you begin to feel a deep appreciation for these people; this sense of gratitude is very humbling and will allow you a self-perception that is very accurate and sincere. You got to where you are today by the assistance of many people that you encountered in your life. You stood on the shoulders of these giants and are a better woman or man because of them.

By reviewing this list and these thoughts, you can prepare your mind to respond in the interview with gratitude when speaking of your past experiences. Your response will trigger feelings and memories of gratitude in the interview panel and endear you to them.

Having answers like this prepared also allows you to convey your strengths and relate the skills you have learned in a strong way, by story relation.

The technique of being complimentary is wise as well, but it is something that must be done with great tact and must be delivered almost imperceptibly. If it isn't genuine, it doesn't sound right so if you can't feel it, don't state it.

—————— ACTION STEP ——————

Pray to God that He gives you insight and wisdom.

CHAPTER 18

STORYTELLING SKILLS

"Your intellect may be confused,
but your emotions will never lie to you."
– Roger Ebert

Story telling is an art in the interview that you should be familiar with. In behaviour based interviewing, you will be asked to tell a story. This gives us the opportunity to express ourselves and cover a topic in-depth, but this should be kept under two minutes max. The stories that you share should be specific, well-constructed and practised prior to the interview so you do not go astray and succumb to the temptation of whatever comes to your mind.

You may be asked to share a story which includes specific examples and may sound something like: "Tell me a time when you were challenged professionally by a co-worker and rose up to the occasion to succeed."

What a great opportunity for you to display exactly what you want them to know about your abilities, or a terrible time to stare blankly at the faces of the interviewers, wondering what the heck you will say next. But if you are not prepared for this line of questioning, this could be the longest part of the interview. If you have nothing to say but stammering clusters of thoughts that are only loosely connected, you will not get a chance to talk about your skills or abilities.

To make sure that this doesn't happen, lay the foundation for any story in the first part. If you are asked about a challenge, make sure it starts with a specific time and place. Create tension right away.

"I was the head waiter at Simons Restaurant during a long winter of no sun …" – give the idea that this was a trying time.

"It was the second day of my new job as a manager and the third person had just resigned ..."

"I was facing some kind of food poisoning as I handled the second biggest client we had ever had ...." These stories can start like this.

In the second part of the story, get to the crisis and successful closure.

"Our biggest customer gave us an ad to run four hours before we were to go to print …"

"My interpreter didn't show up for the meeting with this razor sharp Japanese sales team …"

"My car broke down on the freeway on my way to the biggest closing in the company's history ..."

Remember to keep your stories short and to the point. Introduce the foundation, set up the situation, introduce the challenge and resolve it, all in just a few sentences. Wrap it up with the fact that you were the hero and add any training that you want them to know of. Lastly, give some thought to the subtle ways you could load a story with information that you want them to know.

The main point is to ensure that you are not taken by surprise with this intrusive line of questioning, so be prepared. In your notepad, outline some stories from your professional life using this script. Write out no less than five stories that

INTERVIEW STRATEGY

you will remember when you need to. Make sure to hit all the elements that deliver the message and convey what you learned from this life lesson at the end. Just let it flow, turn off the critic for a while. After they are all down on paper, let them sit a while and do something else.

When you return to the stories, rearrange certain elements of them and edit them until you feel comfortable relating them in a job interview. You could mention something significant about your training, reveal the high level of experience you have, the demanding arena of your profession, or mention your vast management experience if the position requires it. Review the specifications of the job before you go in and select two possible stories that will hit the hot buttons of the job description. The story relates your skills to problem solving and points to direct training that you have received on issues like conflict resolution, perseverance, working under stress and pulling people together.

When going into the story, avoid saying: "Oh, I have a great story for you ..." as this sets up an expectation that may be hard to meet. Imagine talking with a friend and simply telling a situation, in a relaxed tone, and imagine that friend's face watching you with expectation. This is the venue for story telling in the interview and it is a powerful tool to deploy.

When you need to use a personal story, touch on it only briefly and move on. This will demonstrate that you have moved on from the problem. If you would like to take a few moments and look like you are trying hard to think, and are a little uncomfortable diving into your past for a problem, display it. Try to use the same framework and power through the story and again in the end, look to convey your competency, but also a piece of information that reveals the x-factor of how you were able to pull off the event.

A good story teller is always enthralled in his own story and has a passionate need to convey a message in this ancient form of communication. With pen in hand, script out three stories – with no real preparation.

Is everyone born with the mind to recognize what a good opportunity actually looks like? It may be harder than you think. As you are interviewed, you will begin to develop a sharper sense of where you may fit in to work cultures that are different than the one you are working in.

In your *Interview Strategy* notebook, build a picture of what is important to you. What size company would you like to work for? Write down the number of offices and employees that you would like to work for or with. Why is it important? How far will you drive to get to work? Where would you like to appear in the organization chart?

What type of supervisor would you respond to best in a work environment? One that is very involved in the management end of your production or one that keeps out of your way and lets you do your job? If you claim to be the type of person who does not need to be managed, are you quite capable of managing yourself effectively and not giving into distractions, lazy habits or unproductive activity? If you struggle with distraction or lack of motivation, then you cannot manage yourself and, yes, although you are self-employed, you need to be supervised by a client to produce something.

Would you like to supervise people? Imagine the team you would like to manage. Is it a group of whiny busy bodies who can't seem to get along with each other or an elite team of producers that complement each other's strengths and mitigate weaknesses?

What type of goals would you like to be responsible for? Easy results that allow you to be left alone in a cube and unaccountable for anything really, or are you looking for a challenging environment where you can flourish and eat what you kill? Perhaps you want a little bit of both. Write them down in the notebook and build your template.

By looking at what you want, and what you do not want, the template becomes clear. Every few weeks, rewrite your template statement and end it with a vision statement, for example: "The type of position I am looking for will help me gain leverage into a sales management position in the next five years. From the next position I accept, I will be able to see a track to management." Or "In the next five years I will be earning a 200k base salary. The next position I accept will have that potential associated with it."

Clarity is the key to achieving your goals and, when interviewing, you are in fact selecting the team that will work with you. And because you are self-employed and subcontracting your skills out to a company to achieve your objectives, don't forget that your philosophy and your positioning must first serve you. You can really serve no one else unless it does. Develop your template for your future so you can more clearly direct your efforts towards an objective. Practising your interview strategy allows you to realize your potential and maximize your position in life.

——————— ACTION STEP ———————

1. To become more acutely aware of how you spend
    your time, track it precisely in a notebook for three
    days. Then review it with the intention of looking at
    how you can spend it better. Next define what 'Better'
    means to you.

2. Listen to a friend tell a story, hang on the every word
    that they speak and give them your full, undevided
    attention.

CHAPTER 19

YOUR MANAGEMENT STRATEGY

"People don't leave a job, they leave a manager."
— Recruiters' slogan

Are you passionate about leading people? It is one thing to state that you are a manager of people and are good at it, but now be prepared to explain why you are a good manager. Why do you want to be a leader? Who put this desire in you? Did you always have it and were born with it? Perhaps as a kid, on the playground, when it came to follow the leader, you were naturally the leader.

If that is your goal, you would need to develop executive level leadership skills to convince an interviewer that you are the type of manager they want. If you find yourself being drawn to these positions to leap your career forward, know the interviewer will be testing your skills for the high level you are reaching for. What will be vital is your ability to relay your leadership skills in your past employment situations. Look for ways to display yourself as a strong producing manager that has an impressive track record of success in personal production and with the teams you have led. The team that you managed may be studied for functionality, questions may be asked to delve into the condition of the group. They may enquire as to if any of your subordinates went on to become managers themselves. A good tree produces good fruit.

Be prepared to discuss in detail the things you had to get done and include the time frame. Describe the actions of the people that were assigned to you and what was accomplished. Can you persuade others to enlist on your mission with compelling enthusiasm or by tyranny and force? Can you do either if you have to get the job done? Just what is your management philosophy anyway?

Let's get in front of our face plate interview team again. Your management skills are in question.

"What procedures did you implement to improve the process at Spring Cola?" Take a shot at answering the question from the cuff. Then stop, and write down your answer on your notepad. Now write down two more answers, each one a bit more thought out until you have identified direct changes that are honest and impactful. List out the changes; think about how they affected the bottom line and the outcome. Try delivering the answer again, and keep eye contact with the panel.

"What techniques did you utilize to invigorate your team?" the kind face plate asks you. Take an immediate shot at answering the question, stumble through it and get it out there. Freeze everything again and write down the answer you just gave. Look at it and think it through. Answer it twice more in your notebook. Out of the three answers you have just written down, circle the best one.

Now deliver the best answer, naming specific management techniques that you have had training for and speak of the results you achieved in energizing your team. Your own energy should come through when you deliver this answer.

Since this is something you are passionate about, allow yourself to glow with vitality when you speak of the tremendous feeling of satisfaction you gain from watching an elite team work together. Know what your management philosophy is and share it. Speak of how you fostered healthy competition to bring out the best in your team and inspire them with your belief in their abilities. Speak with love, because that is what makes a considerate and talented manager. For this type of leader, the responsibilities of management are never a burden but a pleasure.

"What would subordinates say about you?" angry face plate asks. Give thought to members of your team who were promoted. If someone in your charge went on to better themselves, even to a place in leadership, mention it with pride. They learned it from you so take a bow.

"They might tell you how I never finish a conversation without summarizing what we talked about and what everyone was going to do and achieve by the next weekly meeting. That used to drive them crazy but I noticed they were doing it with each other, and that's when I had a moment of pride." This could be part of your answer.

When interviewing for a serious leadership role, be prepared to be qualified for a specific set of skills that allow you to use courage in decision making. Positions at this level are crucial to hire correctly as this role sets the course for the whole company. Board members lose sleep over these hires; shareholders are waiting with ulcers to see who gets put at the helm of the ship. With so much riding on the line, expect questions that will examine your courage: "Have you ever had to replace key members of a team and what was your procedure?"

"It's never easy. But an evaluation of the team I was taking charge of had to be done quickly. If people can't gel and don't produce, they need to be replaced. It's the bottom 20% rule. The rest of the team you work with feels more elite when the problem people are cut from the roster and they respect you more for it. It may not show right away but it works out that way after a few weeks."

This question could be followed up with: "How would you replace the people you had to let go?"

"I look to the replacement selection internally. If no prospect is found, I might look at the competition and see if there is someone on that team who could be recruited. That not only gets us the ideas we would like but also deals a blow to our competitor.

"If that's not a possibility, I get interviews started and posting out what we are looking for. While we are at it, I might re-evaluate the job description and rewrite some elements of it. We'll also ask as a group, how can we make this position more effective?"

"How do you talk to someone about their weaknesses?" You can outperform your competition by having a good answer for this. Speak about how in your own performance reviews, you felt that if you did not get corrective feedback, you were let down. A good manager is able to tell you what you are not doing right and where you need to work. If it's just a pleasure fest for a review, no one is growing and improving, so it's a waste of time. Speak like that to answer the question, so that you avoid going off on a rabbit trail.

"What is the most important part of hiring someone?" the face plate to your right asks you.

"Well, first of all, I study that position inside and out; to make sure I have a good grasp on the most essential parts of the job criteria. If I don't fully understand the job requirements, then I won't be able to qualify it in a good candidate, or be able to gauge if they have achieved it in the past. I look for them to seek to understand the position themselves so that we can both speak to the outcome together. I try to define the job in forms of non-negotiable criteria, then I know I am ready to interview someone."

The answer might seem a bit general, but at first that is a safe bet. If they want more details, they will ask drill down questions from there.

At the senior level, the questions of who you might hire are relevant; make a mistake not hiring the right talent and you affect the flight of the ship. Do you hire people who are non-threatening to you because you are insecure in your future? If you did, this would have you frightened to hire skilled candidates because they would make you look bad or could replace you. There are managers who think this way.

Speak to how you hire people who are smarter than you and then listen to them. Speak to how you expect someone on your staff to supersede you one day in ability and authority because nothing stands still. Confidently speak of how one of your theories is to train someone who is a subordinate to be able to replace you, should the day come when you yourself move on.

Speak it from your heart; the truth has a ring to it that people can't help but be affected by. Others in the room will feel your honesty and understand you better. Speaking in this gut level truth is how difficult interview panels are won over, with intellect but with emotion. End with the premise that because that performance review changed your direction, you now believe that a manager has a responsibility to give corrective feedback to subordinates as it can save their jobs and careers. The trick is to do it with tact. What interferes with the natural execution of your verbal communication is excessive nervousness. Again, the more prepared you are, the easier it will be to keep the butterflies at bay.

When the interview feels like it is getting personal, remember that it is not. Sometimes an interview can feel like an inquisition and, rather than qualifying you, it suddenly feels like the panel is only trying to disqualify you. But if you can't be disqualified, you are, by default, qualified. Only, it is not as fun and pleasant. This does not mean that this hiring manager is evil or mean; it just means this person has a different style of communication that has possibly served him or her well. An aggressive interview style can take place for a short period of time within an interview, or it may be the entire length of the meeting. They are done deliberately for any number of reasons. Here are a few:

1. They have enough candidates for the position and do not feel the need to recruit anyone for the role, so coddling candidates is not going to happen; they want to know who will stay when it gets hot in the kitchen.

2. The interview team itself has a dramatic contrasting dynamic to it, a cowboy who wants to show off to the ladies or a lady who feels like she needs to be super stern to impress the men. Any imbalance of social factors can cause this phenomenon, and with a growing sense of group think, they all converge on some candidates and attack in a pack. Most of them would deny it happened afterwards.

3. They filled the position recently and the hire was there for three weeks and washed out when the stress levels got high. The interview team has now decided to apply

some stress to the candidates to see if they can cut it before they make another offer.

The questions will be direct and be delivered without any sweetener. For example: "What makes you think you can apply for a role managing 13 people when your only experience is mentoring two co-workers?" When a question like this comes up, pay attention to the set up. The question was: "What makes you think ..." so speak to the set up.

"I think I can do that because I am a natural leader. And yes, I have mentored two co-workers but those co-workers succeeded greatly under my guidance. I connect with people and inspire them with my own enthusiasm. You could hire someone with more management background but you won't get the results that I can with my infectious ambition." Wait a moment for the team to acknowledge your complete answer, then fire back a missile of your own.

"While we are on the subject, why did the last manager only stay for four months before moving on?" Ask your own direct, elephant in the room question, and do it with a pleasant, relaxed, professional tone.

It is important that at some point you not only receive the tough question, answer it well, but then return one of your own. Conversations can be fierce and productive if front-loaded and framed correctly.

By handling tough questions with a cool head, you supersede all other candidates and stand out quickly in the most effective way. The interview team accomplishes their objective as well, identifying candidates who have the salt to lead in a tough environment.

They may very well like you and not know why. The reason is you took what they had to offer and gave it back to them with style, and at the end of it smiled and closed them down on the job like a peer. If you handle this test correctly, there is a chance you could have a seat at their table. It could be the very thing they are looking for in candidates, so let out your own warrior and qualify them as well.

———————— ACTION STEP ————————

1. Select a soft cover binder and label it 'Management Strategy'. Fill it with a collection of techniques, products and communications that serve to intensify your own ability to lead and inspire people around you.

2. Organize the binder weekly, moving paper thoughts around to gain a comprehensive philosophy that you can express to others, with your real-life experiences.

3. Give a presentation on this topic to anyone who will listen – an empty room if you have to – on a monthly basis until you are good at it.

CHAPTER 20

REVIEWING
THE NOTEBOOK

"There is a place here that only you can fill."
– Michael McLean

It's time to review the notebook and look at what you have written down. Study the notes and thoughts, examine the concerns, fears and considerations that are truly only yours. There is bliss in growth and if you should feel it as you glance back down the road you have been walking, let it settle on you for a moment. These feelings will give you tremendous confidence in times of pressure. And if you should find yourself suddenly unemployed, all these interviews will be a fantastic resource for you to draw on. It will happen automatically. By taking these actions you have left your old self behind and taken on a journey of growth.

Now we can also write: "What questions can I ask to uncover concerns with the hiring authority before I leave the interview?"

- Is there a certain skill set that you are looking for that is the key to this hire?

- As you look at my background, are there any concerns that you would like to address with me before I leave?

- Do you have any concerns about my background that may eliminate me from consideration?

- Here are three statements I can make about my past that will speak to my stability.

- I value straightforward communication and results in goal-setting. I invite you to look for it in my actions.

- I consider myself dependable and tenacious; I believe my peers and co-workers would say that about me.

- I understand how important it is to commit to results and an organization for the duration. If you look at some of the points on my résumé, I believe you will find a stable consistency.

In examining what is happening we can pin some things together that will help you move forward through the interview process with better momentum. As you evaluate the positions you have interviewed for thus far, did you really understand the position well? Did you know what you were applying for? Did you ask the hiring manager the right questions to uncover any facts that would move you forward in the process?

A skill in interviewing for positions is being able to interview the hiring panel to determine whether the position is a good fit for you. Be thankful for any positions you went into that were not a good fit, because if you study them, you may learn what questions you should have asked.

——————————— ACTION STEP ———————————

Ask a friend to interview you and then get his or her opinion on how you did. Ask what you could do to improve.

CHAPTER 21

SEEING AND BEING READY FOR ANY OPPORTUNITY

> *"You are a child of God.*
> *Your playing small doesn't serve the world."*
> — Marianne Williamson

As you think about interviewing, and begin to see it in a new light with a relaxed attitude of studied preparation, you may see it as a game. And isn't everything really? Games are fun. When you play a game, sometimes you win and sometimes you lose. You have become unafraid of failure because exposure decides your life and provides you with options that have always been yours, though you did not see them.

With each interview, you gain more experience at recognizing a good opportunity. You also open up your network and can examine the professional world around you. At the same time, you are learning a great deal about people and how they build teams and hire the right talent to make a fantastic machine of human potential.

One of the circumstances you might encounter is a newly created position. Sometimes this unfolds as you are interviewing for one position and the hiring manager mentions in the interview that they have a new opening, or there is another position that you might consider. He may describe it briefly and ask if you are interested in this.

Good companies do this; they hire good people and then sometimes figure out exactly where they want them. If this is what they are doing, it can be a good thing. But it will be necessary for you to determine the standing of your chances for the initial position you were interviewing for. Probe back to that through the process while learning all you can about the new position.

Sometimes newly created positions are problematic. You need to ask some questions to find out how serious they are about filling it. Does the person asking you if you are interested in moving forward with this position really have the authority to pull the trigger on a hire? Is this a separate department with a different hiring authority? Here are some points to consider:

- What is the process for applying for this new position? Asking this question may reveal who else will be involved in the subsequent interview. The higher up in the company chart, the better the likelihood that it has momentum.

- What are the standards of performance measurement? Asking this question will reveal the level of planning and design put on the new position. It will also give you that critical knowledge with regards to stepping into a situation that will foster your success or set you up for the chopping block on unreal expectations.

- What are the tools you will use? Are there up-to-date systems and technology or support staff to assist you, or are you a one person show?

- Are there promotional opportunities with this position? Five years from now where will you be with the company if you do this role very well?

- Have they interviewed anyone else for the role? What makes your skills specifically a good fit?

- If there is a first place contender for the original position you are now interviewing for, will you be circled back to for consideration if the first place contender doesn't accept or is that option really dead?

- What is the compensation range like for the role? Is there a bonus to be awarded for job performance? What are the pay-out numbers?

- In speaking to the hiring manager about this role, use a high level of tact to extract the answers to the questions and set up the question when necessary with a front-loading statement. Be agreeable and friendly while intensely focused.

Avoid agreeing to accept any position until you have a chance to go home and consider it overnight. Ask yourself if the curve ball position fits your desired career path and utilizes your skills. Is it a financial and professional move forward for you? An hour ago, you did not know this position existed; be clear in asking yourself if you want it. Does your gut tell you this is a fabulous and exciting opportunity? Then you are on the right path.

——————————— ACTION STEP ———————————

1. Interview anyone you find yourself in conversation with. Take a genuine interest in their background, their ambitions, hopes and dreams. Try to determine what their strengths are and where they may need improvement. Do this without being obvious, but leave the person with a feeling that you cared about them.

2. Study the impact that this has on your relationship with them.

CHAPTER 22

MORE TECHNIQUES

*"If everything is under control,
you are not going fast enough."*
– Mario Andretti

A system for fielding and answering questions can be helpful in handling this pressure. A basic strategy for receiving and responding to multiple questions is FFOQC. Say it – FFOQC! Repeat it a few times until it rolls off your tongue. This stands for Front-load, Fact, Opinion, Qualifications and Close. For example, with the question: "How would your peers describe you?"

Front-load: "Well, I'm not one who frequently speaks the mind of others, because anytime we do, we speak only of our own perceptions about what those people might be thinking. I can only give you my perception and estimation."

Fact: "I can tell you factually that in my last day at my last job, they threw me a party at the Olive Garden. My technical support person gave me a rubber hand exercise ball that I would take off her desk and squeeze when we were under pressure; she told me that I had a tremendous impact on her career development and I had inspired her to grow in data research because she now felt it a vital function to the company. My credit administrator cried and asked me again not to leave and she is also one of my referees."

Opinion: "But I think they would tell you that I work all day on the top priority assignments and waste no production time on meaningless things. I take my work very seriously and hold back nothing. I go the extra mile and get the job done while keeping spirits high around me. That is what I hope they would say and I can tell you that I have worked very hard to have that be my legacy."

Qualification: "I feel that my background in managing a sales floor has given me a unique ability to relate to people under stressful situations and pull them together, and this is what you will hear when checking my references."

Close: "I know that the position I am interviewing with you for has a strong mentorship aspect to it, and blends a performance foundation with leadership, and that is who I am. Have I perceived the position correctly?"

By following a structured formatted response, and systemizing your ability to present answers, you will consistently be able to communicate your strengths and ideas more profoundly, no matter how many questions you have to answer in a day.

If the hiring authority is seeking idealistic answers, or seems to be digging for your intellectual responses to abstract questions and ideas, use the word 'think' in your answer. Begin sentences with "I think ..." when you feel that your thinking is being examined.

If you are being asked a great deal of emotionally charged questions, begin sentences with, "I feel that ...". This will help you appear to identify with the question and convey that you clearly understand the line of questioning and can follow the train of thought.

DESC: Direct, Explain, Specifics and Close (or Desk as I call it) is another method of receiving, processing and responding to a question. When a question is very blunt, the interviewer wants you to lower your guard and talk about the elephant in the room. If the hiring authority has this strategy in his interview style, be grateful. In all of these procedures we all long to be treated as equals, with honesty and understanding. A direct question sometimes deserves a direct answer.

If the invitation to drop the contest and really connect should present itself, the question may sound like this: "What can you do for my company?"

Direct: "I can increase your bottom line in the first six months I'm here." Only say this, of course, if you can do it and have thought it out.

Explain: "If you hire me, my knowledge of tax law will allow me to maximize the department to all breaks that are within the law and I can, most often, save you money."

Specifics: "At my last two places, I increased the bottom line. At Wellington Research I gained them 39% in profits, just from what I was able to redirect. At Pembroke, it was more like 29% but an increase in the bottom line is like gold."

Then, like all answers, **close** it up: "I can do that for you if you give me the opportunity."

If you're asked a pesky negative answer question, when the hiring manager is politely asking you to disqualify yourself in the interview by asking you to say something heinous about yourself (so that you can make his job easier and he can yell "Next!"), roll an opposite into the answer to neutralize the negative: "Can you give me an example of a time when you did not relate well to someone?" When you feel compelled to answer questions like this, roll in a statement that presents you in an opposing way.

"I was new to a management role, and was promoted out of the work crew because of my performance, to lead the team. This immediately changed the relationship with my co-workers. When I had to step up as a leader, some of them related to me as a co-worker and forced my hand so that I had to enact disciplinary measures and change the work relationship. It was a mistake for me to think that I could be both a buddy, co-worker and a manager and I learned a hard lesson then."

--------------------- **ACTION STEP** ---------------------

1. Review your *Interview Strategy* notebook with a high-lighter in your hand. Look for landmark thoughts of developed thinking in your language. Look at what you took on, who you met and what you accomplished as far as networking and expanding your options in life. Allow a sense of accomplishment to well up within you.

2. Ask yourself, what will you take on next?

3. Trouble shooting: in your *Interview Strategy* notebook, make a list, from your gut, raw and real, about the potential hot spots that could flare up in your interview.

CHAPTER 23

PROBABILITY THEORY

> *"If you are not willing to risk the unusual,*
> *you will have to settle for the ordinary."*
> — Jim Rohn

Interviewing is a shake of the dice. What we are initiating and utilizing is probability theory; the more opportunities you examine, the higher number of opportunities you will be exposed to. The more decisions you make, the better you get at decision-making. Sure, there will be some bad experiences and some interviews that don't go so well. So what? It will only have the weight you decide to give it.

By reviewing your goals and your *Interview Strategy* notebook daily, you will be able to examine your own strengths and weaknesses which will help you to focus. This will help you to keep your mind away from activities that may disturb your energy.

This brings us to the most critical part of the interview process, the decision-making part. The pressure is undoubtedly immense and can flare up your ulcer, cost you sleep and have you staring at the grass in the back yard as the kids wonder what has gotten into you. This sounds bad and stressful, but it shouldn't be. The fun in choosing your destiny is that you get to reap the benefits of courageous decisions that only you can make. You will learn to love it. You are to be a career developer and a sojourner in the world of the professional. You see it as a war campaign and own the results of your efforts, as they will certainly be gold.

When considering your decision-making strategy, look at the Meta-decision. This is a decision that will decide how you make this decision. Think about what boundaries you will use to make this decision, how long you will spend making it and what key factors you will allow into its frame. Also consider if you need to make this decision at all.

Deciding how you will decide is the Meta-decision. This will prevent you from diving into something without a decision-making process. In your notebook write down the main factors that are vital to what you want to achieve. The purpose for this career change is going to be based on these three key elements, for example:

1.   Career advancement

2.   More money

3.   Less commute time

These are critical points that need to be addressed in this decision. What is the crux of the issue? You should continually ask yourself and answer in writing. This answer could change as you re-write it.

A decision frame will have to be built and stood on. This frame is the set of standards and facts that you will use to structure your decision. It is a template. Anytime we make a decision we create a frame and then use it to see the opportunity, issue and problem, whatever. The frame allows you to highlight what you are labelling as important. So, glance at it once in a while to see what you are not using in your decision frame and re-evaluate it to make sure it is not important and does not have a place in the frame.

Having this process in place will prevent you from depending too much on intuition. Sometimes, you may feel that you have made a critical decision based on emotions that were erroneous and unsound. Ouch. The drawback of intuitive decision making is that it is scientifically inconsistent.

The Ben Franklin method of making a decision consisted of making two lists on one page. A list of pros and cons that can be compared. Each pro can be cancelled out with a con. If he had more pros, he would then choose in favour of that decision. On the other hand, if there were more cons, he would go against the decision. This technique is just a way of thinking on paper and evaluating options. There is something concrete about being able to look at the guts of your options written before you in your own hand and weighing them with your mind.

Decision making is a skill that improves with development. As all skills are learned and therefore learnable, we must remember to welcome the pressure and move forward with the results, seeing all processes through to the end.

If you decide to turn down a job and opt for another one, or decide to stay where you are, regard your decision-making experience highly and don't look back or beat yourself up afterwards. If you do make a mistake, remember that is what needs to be done to train you to make effective decisions. Framing the correct information and preventing blindness of certain facts and data is vital.

If you do make a mistake, learn from it and incorporate it into your process. In practising sound decision-making strategies, beware of fear as a motivator to do or not do something. Every decision that is made fearfully is usually framed falsely and lacks vision, depth and self-trust.

—————————— ACTION STEP ——————————

Write out a paragraph defining success in your terms. List five reasons why you should succeed. Write how achieving this would improve and change your life. List five companies that may be able to help you achieve this goal if you worked for them. These are your target companies to get interviews with.

CHAPTER 24

REALIZING YOUR AMBITIONS

"sometimes intense desire creates it's own talent."
– Eric Hoffer

Ambition is a good thing. It's like desire. It shows itself when people are passionate about what they are doing. Desire adds flames to personal relationships and gives every protagonist in a story something to go after. It's OK to want something. There is no wrong in it. Give yourself permission to succeed.

Your *Interview Strategy* notebook has become more than just a journal of a personal voyage of discovery. Because you have strategized and thought of the future, it is the foundation of a fantastic business plan. You have built a vision, and this vision will become your mission and introduce opportunities and people into your life that will help you achieve your goals. Interviewing is communication, and this is one of our fundamental requirements for achieving success.

Use visualization techniques that professional athletes use daily. Take a few moments each day to hold a picture in your mind of you doing well in an interview. You easily answer questions in a professional tone and convey ideas clearly, so that people understand your skills and strengths. By training your mind to see opportunity, you will recognize it when others won't. By making yourself think optimistically, you can train your thought process and redirect your life's results. By focusing on your objectives and working to make them happen, you can make yourself happy. Your goal should always be to be content where you are. Enjoy the company of those around you and also keep a long-term perspective about where you are working.

The techniques discussed in this book will increase your ability to communicate your ambitions to others and create a synergy of exploration in your life and the lives of anyone you touch with this power. With a change in attitude about your career development, a high standard of knowledge and performance in anything you do and the ability to communicate that, you will never need to fear a change of direction in your career.

As you conclude this book, I hope you have become more aware of the personal power you possess, and this doubles your career expectations to the point that you become financially independent through a life committed to principle, development, ambition and kindness. Nothing can stop you now and really, it never could.

Sometimes things go right in the interview and sometimes things go wrong. The art of executing your interview strategy is to roll with what happens and realize that sometimes things go wrong. Roll with it, don't think much about it. Write it down in your notebook if you must, if you think that you have learned something from it and wish not to repeat it.

INTERVIEW OUTTAKES

As an executive recruiter, with sixteen years of helping people make career changes and recruiting top level people for incredible opportunities, I have seen or stood next to people who have dealt with some incredible things. Here are a few memories from candidates on interviews:

- A candidate answered a cell phone call from his boss and talked to him for five minutes in the middle of an interview. Then fell asleep in the car ride with the hiring authority to the airport. Guess what, he got the job!

- A candidate asked so many questions of the hiring panel it became comical. He didn't pick up on it until he kept firing questions and they were almost rolling on the floor laughing.

- A candidate showed up at 5:00 am for the interview instead of 5:00 pm.

- A candidate jokingly told his interviewer that if he got the job, and had to move to the state, he would not become a Hawkeye fan. The hiring authority walked out of the room in anger, not to return. The candidate had to drive back the four hours, wondering what had happened.

- The candidate's spouse insisted on going to the interview and sat in through the meeting, refusing to leave. The meeting was short and tense.

- In a dinner meeting, which the candidate's wife was also invited too, the wife got drunk and insulted the hiring authority.

- A candidate was flown in for an interview and put up in a hotel room. The hiring manager dropped by the hotel room unannounced to introduced himself and the candidate answered the door drunk and in his underwear.

- In an attempt to impress executives in a bank, a candidate spouted personal financial information out about customers he had attracted to his previous company, a violation of client privacy. They passed on him.

- A candidate showed up at the wrong company, got an interview and was offered a job.

- A candidate received an offer for a position in her first interview. She accepted it and the interviewer made a pass at her. She told him to stick his offer and left the room.

- A woman wore a certain type of perfume and everyone in the room sneezed so much they had to end the interview.

So, whatever happens, the good reasons for getting out there and meeting the most effective people in your industry always outweigh the bad. And, if the bad should happen, laugh at it, and move on.

CONCLUSION

Now "the world is your oyster". This expression comes from Shakespeare's play *The Merry Wives of Windsor* (1600) when Pistol is told by Flagstaff that he, "Will not lend him a penny." Pistol replies, "Why, then the world is mine oyster, which I with sword will open." It appears that Pistol will take charge of his own fate and will use a little muscle to find the pearl (wealth).

I've found a few different definitions of what this expression may mean:

1. An opportunity is open to someone, and the world is theirs to enjoy.

2. In order to achieve something in this world, one has to grab opportunity.

I like the second expression. It is the premise of this book. Is it fair to yourself and your family to ignore those options and put your head down, and to take only what you stumble on with hardly looking? When we reach the end of our days, will we look back at the splendour and daring that we took on and crafted our fortune with, or will we wonder what could have been?

By taking charge of your career development and an active stance towards the future, you shake off a troubling apprehension that is telling you that you are wasting time. In those reflective moments, sometimes we glance in the rear view mirror and see what we could have been if we would have had more insight. What might have been if we would have tried harder?

We don't even have to try hard to escape that fate, just try at all. Perhaps that's enough. Will we listen to the voice of fear telling us to stay put, or stride nervously for the first time into a life changing interview? By becoming a skilled interviewee, you have elevated your communication style to a level that has allowed you to recognize, explore and obtain options rather than bounce off of them. By handling fear of change the only way there is, head on, the future suddenly holds more possibilities than it did before. This has given you a new sense of confidence in yourself and the future you have the ability to create.

If your company sells now, because you are the CEO of your own personal services corporation, you will be able to handle finding a new client. You know the other companies in your space, and you know who to talk to and what it is like to have an executive conversation with them about their needs and your future, and can determine if there is a match.

You have gained an exploratory view of the employment landscape for miles around. Those hiring managers remember meeting you, and because you were well prepared and knew how to communicate your skills, desires and requirements, they know what they need to do to get a hold of you and recruit you to their team. You never know when that will pay off.

By practising techniques of enquiry and exposition, you can properly relate your strengths and match them to an organization's needs. And you have learned to do this by practising in the theatre of the real. The people that you have encountered will know and remember you. When you see them at a function, you will have standing ground with them.

The threat of losing your job is something that has faded away and will not be back. You are ahead of it. You are too busy evaluating your options expertly and leveraging your career forward to take the threat of being left out in a merger seriously. You like the people you work with but are not about to waylay your career because you want to hang out with your friends. You have a career to tend to. The decision-making mechanism in your mind is growing in strength and ability. You ask key, probing questions when exploring options, when examining options that deal with the crux of any issue. The elephant in the room is talked about in a comfortable and tactful manner when you are in a meeting.

This has left a lasting and profound effect on the people you encounter. As a result you stand out against the candidates who are interviewing in the hiring process who compete with you. Because you have rehearsed answering and asking questions, and presenting your skill sets, your language is powerful and concise, your delivery tactful. This has led to other advantages in your life that you are beginning to experience.

With your family, you are confident about the future and relaxed; this feeling, like all feelings, is contagious. Now your decisions are not hemmed in and restricted by fear. Learning to interview has become a career development tool that has cleared up other areas of your life and taught you decision-making skills at the highest level. It has become a self-development tool and has removed doubt from your perception and given you a new idea of what this world and your life has to offer.

Any time we do not meet something head on and duck it, it extends its grip on us. You no longer fear change – now you create it, manage it and are on your way to mastering it. That is, if you are prepared to take it by sword. Perhaps the violent connotation is something we should remember to keep about the world being your oyster. You have to pick up the clam and open it with your knife if you have to.

So, go take what is yours in this word. It has always been yours. You are unstoppable.

Sample questions:

1. Why do you want this job?

2. Tell me about yourself.

3. Why do you want to leave your current employer?

4. Have you signed a non-compete agreement?
    Would you sign one here if we hired you?

5. How do you plan your days?

6. In what ways has your self motivation shown itself in your life?

7. In what ways have you been successful in life?

8. Have you been successful in your personal life as well?

9. What has been your favourite job? Why?
    Do you regret leaving there?

10. Please give me an example of a time when you took instructions well.

11. How do you feel about doing work that is repetitious?

12. What do you know about our company?

13. What is your theory of the concept of delayed gratification? Have you practised this theory in your life? How?

14. At your current company, who is the top performer? What traits does this person have?

15. Please describe a day on the job in your current situation. What part is most rewarding to you?

16. What were the last two books you read?

17. How did you pay for college?

18. Tell me about the first job you ever had. How old were you?

19. What led you into this industry? Is this what you studied in school?

20. What are your salary requirements? What are you making now? When was your last raise?

21. What is the biggest challenge in your industry? How do you prepare for the next?

22. Where do you see yourself in five years?

23. Tell me a story where you had to use people skills to solve a problem during the work day.

24. What are your top three accomplishments in life?

25. What are you particularly proud of?

26. What continued education have you engaged in since college?

27. How do you approach goal setting?

28. What particular skills do you have that will make you do this job well?

29. Sell me this pen.

30. How many hours do you think someone should work in a week?

31. Do you have any vacations planned this year already?

32. What would you prefer your next job title to be?

33. Do you have management experience?
    What is your management philosophy?

34. How far is the commute from your house to this office?
    How do you feel about that?

35. What do you require from an employer?

36. What type of work environment do you prefer to work in?

37. What would your peers say about you?
    How about your last two supervisors?

38. How do you spend your free time?
    What is your favourite day of the week?

39. Do you have any concerns about your ability to do this job?

40. When have you done it before and for how long?

41. What can we expect from you?

42. What question are you hoping I don't ask?
    (Always a big smile behind this one.)

43. What is your philosophy about humour in the office?

44. What are your career goals?

45. What was your GPA in college?

46. Tell me why you left the last three companies you worked for.

47. How do you approach decision making?

48. Do you have any regrets in life?

49. Who are the most important people in your life?

50. How long have you been considering this change in your career?

51. What specifically are you looking for in your next career move?

52. Something seems wrong, what is it?

53. What tough decisions have you had to make in the last year?

54. Who is your favourite author?

55. What year has been your highest level of performance? What made that happen?

56. Are you motivated by promotional awards for performance?

57. Are you people or technically oriented?

58. What type of manager do you like to work for?

59. In what ways are you active in your community?

60. How do you work under pressure? Examples please.

61. If you were the CEO of the company you work for, what would you change?

62. Have you considered the possibility that your current employer will offer you a raise to stay?
What will you do then?

63. What kind of offer are you looking for?
No, I am not talking about a cup of coffee.

64. What clubs do you belong to?

65. What are your strengths? Weaknesses?

66. Would you say that you are organized?

67. What time do you like to get to work?

68. How do you plan to excel in this profession?

69. Do you have references? Who are they from?

70. Do you have any questions for me?

71. Do you feel like I am the type of boss you can work for?

AN INTRODUCTION TO
JIM FINUCAN

Jim Finucan is the Founder, President and CEO of Tactical Search & Recruitment, a firm that specializes in recruitment in the banking sector.